YOUR BEST BRAIN

*When Life Knocks You Down,
Calmly Get Up, Smile and Say
'You Hit Like a Bitch'*

DR. TERALYN SELL (PHD)

ACKNOWLEDGEMENTS

I have such immense gratitude for so many people who inspire me every single day and who inspired me to get this book out to the world.. Just thinking about you all makes my heart swell and my eyes misty.

The first person I want to thank with all my heart is my forever person, my biggest fan, my husband, Steve. You have been my voice of reason when I felt weak, my source of encouragement when doubt clouded my mind, and my biggest cheerleader when I accomplished something new. Your unwavering support has been my anchor, and I know without it, I wouldn't have made it this far. I look forward to everything life has in store for us, knowing we'll face it together. Words will never fully capture how much I love and appreciate you— but I hope these ones come close.

To my incredible kiddos, Mickayla, Taylor, and Kaiden: you are my favorite people in the world and my greatest joy. Everything I do in life is driven by my love for you. Each of you is so beautifully unique, and I treasure those differences more than I can express. You've each taught me important lessons about life, love, and resilience. But most of all, I hope you're proud of who you are because I couldn't be prouder to be your mom.

To my granddaughter, Baby B: You brought a spark into my life when I didn't even know I needed it. You've taught me to see the world differently, to let go of the small things, and to simply be. Your fire and spirit inspire me every day, and my deepest hope is that you'll always carry that light within you, no matter what this world throws your way.

To my mom and dad: I did it! I've come to understand that my achievements never needed your approval to be worthy, and your love was always there, even when it wasn't spoken aloud. Mom, I see you and understand you now in ways I couldn't before. Dad, I miss you more than words can say.

To Grandpa Steve: I miss our long coffee-fueled conversations so much. When Grandma Faye passed, you taught me the first law of thermodynamics, and at the time, I didn't fully grasp its meaning. Now I do—energy never truly disappears, it just transforms. I feel you with me still, and I know we'll meet again.

To my forever friend, Chris: Two superheroes, no sidekicks. That's us. If we have a piece of wood and some time, we can build anything—just like we've built a friendship that has spanned decades. You've been my steady light, my sounding board, and my sister in every way that counts. Thank you for always being there.

To Cali: You are the friend who, with just one phone call, would be on a plane without hesitation. Your heart is enormous, and your personality even bigger. You've been a constant source of encouragement, cheering me on to finish this book (and so much more). Thank you for always showing up, in every way that matters.

And now, let's wipe away the tears (seriously, get a tissue), grab a cup of coffee, and dive into this book. The sentimental stuff is over—for now—so let's get down to business.

TABLE OF CONTENTS

INTRODUCTION

The amount of times that I have been prescribed psychiatric medications is astounding for one person. I say that because for a while every time I went to the doctor and 'complained' about something (mostly fatigue BTW), I was offered psych meds. Each time I was offered a medication I was in a difference stage of what I call my personal and professional awakening period. One, building off of the next. Throughout this book I will trickle in my personal story in hopes that there is something relatable for you there.

ANXIETY

I distinctly remember thinking I was absolutely going crazy!

I will never forget the worst time I had experienced anxiety. I was a therapist, but I was stuck in a shit job. It wasn't the clients that were causing the problems for me, it was the staff. I had never experienced this type of bullying in my life. It felt like everywhere I turned another rumor was circulating about me. I was beside myself with pain. That pain turned to anxiety in the worst way.

I didn't want to get up and go to work in the morning. I would go to bed overthinking strategy for the next day. I would run through fictitious scenarios over and over again in my mind. My brain seemed like it could never shut the fuck up! I would have courageous conversations (in my head) that would never happen in real life. I felt cut off at the knee caps at work. I felt like I was going crazy.

During the work day I thought I was keeping my shit together, but I wasn't. I was closing myself in my office. I would have cement shoes on that kept me from leaving my office 'sanctuary' unless I absolutely had to. I started becoming afraid of opening emails and taking phone calls, always worried about what I was going to read or who was on the other end of the phone to chew me out. It was Ludacris!

At the end of every night I would race to my car, get in and start to cry. I cried hard night after night. I would yell on the way home…yell at them, whomever 'they' were. Again having these crazy conversations just to get it all out. I remember crying so hard that the tears burned out of my eyes. My vision was blurry half the time and I often wondered if I should actually be driving as I gripped the wheel even harder. Some nights, however, I was numb….so numb. I couldn't even remember the ride home. I was lost in my head, in those damn scenarios.

The entire commute was only 8 minutes door to door. That wasn't a lot of time to do anything about my emotions. But, I would turn into my drive way and shove it all inside of me. It was time for me to be a mom, a wife. I didn't have time to deal with being crazy. I had shit to do. Like a flip of a switch I was someone else. Someone I thought everyone wanted me to be. Until bedtime came and the entire damn process started over again and again.

I knew I had to do something to change this. Something drastic….but what?

Hi there! I'm Dr. Teralyn (PhD) and I have spent the better part of my career engrossed in helping people who struggle with mental health and addiction problems feel better faster. I wasn't always a therapist gone rogue. At first, as a psychotherapist, I was a good steward to psychiatry and learning how we can make new neurological connections through traditional therapy. I am skilled in addiction treatment, EMDR trauma treatment and now I continue to be in hot pursuit of how to influence brain health. I am still a therapist serving local clients, but my exclusive brain health program can be used across the country! I am a self-professed control freak and have juggled everything and then some. I started my Master's Degree in Counseling when I had a 1 year old, 7 year old and a 12 year old. I also had 3 daycare centers that my hubby and I owned. By the time I finished with my PhD in Psychology I had an 11 year old, 17 year old and 22 year old. Crazy right? I kept it all going until fatigue and anxiety took the wheel…but, I still made everything look easy and I know you do too. Throughout this book I will share my story and I will share bits and bites of how you can kick anxiety to the curb. Enough about me because, now its about you…

You make everything look so damn easy…

You get up in the morning, fly around the house getting everyone where they need to be while pouring yourself the last few drops of luke warm coffee. Your ride to work often includes the realization that you forgot your own lunch, again because you were too busy worrying about everyone else you forgot about yourself. You've climbed the ranks in your job, have a couple of kids that you adore

and a spouse that loves you. You keep trudging along every day…
day after day.

But, you've got a dirty little secret…

You secretly wonder if you are enough, constantly. Your job is
intense, the kids are needy and your spouse doesn't really 'see' you.
You make it look perfect on the outside so nobody would ever
know that something is wrong on the inside. Your anxiety is
through the roof every day. You worry that one day you will be
'found out', exposed for being a fraud. So you continuously strive
for more in an attempt to prove yourself.

You've got a dirty little secret her name is anxiety or depression, and
she's a real bitch!

It's time for a YOUR BEST BRAIN

This book is a culmination of ideas and solutions to help you kick
anxiety and depression to the curb. If you are anything like I was
you are looking for solutions that will work. You are looking to
regain your life without more medication or endless hours of talk
therapy.

Do you want to eliminate the stress and anxiety that continues to
weigh you down, make you feel like you're on a never-ending roller
coaster? Does it feel like you can never get caught up? That your
world continues to get more complex, more out of control?

I can't think of a professional or a stay-at-home parent these days
who does not have some negative stress affecting their life right now
and is seeking some peace and relief. Of course, you've tried your

best to keep everything in order, calm and moving forward. I know you have been doing the best you can, but for some reason that never seems to be good enough.

Who wouldn't want to eliminate the overwhelm which seems to always build to the point where you can't even breathe?

Have you noticed that people in your office or in your social circles seem to have it all together, even though they are dealing with a similar giant "To-Do" list every day? But despite your best efforts, it may seem like you can't get caught up and you're always behind, exhausted, and running out of hours at the end of the day.

There are a lot of myths, misconceptions and misinformation out there about what it takes to a handle on your stress and anxiety. It may seem like it should be an easy and quick fix, maybe just a pill, right? But it's rarely that simple…

However, it's essential for maintaining or recovering your health, both physical and mental. If things continue as they have been, you know it will not be a pretty picture, shit is going to hit the fan at some point.

How many times have you seen others seemingly find that peace and happiness you are so desperately seeking? Like they have found the answer or a magic genie in a bottle?

Have you ever talked to friends or your spouse about what you're experiencing, and they just don't seem to understand? They just don't get it, do they, and for some reason they can brush off the feelings of constant overwhelm and dissatisfaction with your life, career, relationships, and more.

Do you struggle with even wanting to get out of bed because of the crushing weight of what you feel you need to accomplish every day, that you don't even know where to begin?

You've probably been told to just relax, have a drink, take a vacation, or maybe that it's just life and life is hard. Maybe you've even gone to your doctor and told them about your issues. They listened intently and then prescribed you some medication to get you 'straightened out', feeling better. When you asked how long you would have to take the pills, they said, "Well, we'll cross that bridge when we get there. We'll talk about that when the time is right." But, the time is never right. As a matter of fact you feel quite paralyzed with the non-answers and the endless battle to get off your medication. So you continue to trudge through life.

But you've been on those vacations. You've had those drinks. And you've been taking the pills for a long, long time, maybe even adding some more to the cocktail. Or, changing dosing, changing medication, yet that is the only thing that actually changes.

And none of it has worked. In fact, you feel even worse than before. More stressed, more overwhelmed, more…shitty. Or worse, you feel numb, disconnected and libido, what in the hell is that?

Now you're feeling like, "Wow, there's something terribly wrong with me that I need all of this medication or alcohol or whatever just to survive as a human. And I don't even feel like I'm surviving, much less thriving."

You are not alone. A lot of people, approximately 8.3 million Americans, are experiencing life-threatening and seriously debilitating psychological distress every day. They're feeling that they are stuck in a world that gets harder to navigate all the time, that for them, the overwhelm will never go away. And they just want to end their pain and misery.

Think about it, our world continues to get more complicated and faster paced all the time. The pressures of family life, work life, social life, and trying to find some time for self-care have been building for years.

The impact of stress-related illness has been well-documented by dozens of studies. Researchers have found stress seems to worsen or increase the risk of conditions like obesity, heart disease, Alzheimer's disease, diabetes, depression, gastrointestinal problems, and asthma.

And it's not going away any time soon. You don't have to look very far to see that more people than ever before are stressed, depressed and anxiety-ridden, and many are unable to get the help they need.

A recent study concluded that mental illness is on the rise and suicide is on the rise. And access to care for the mentally ill is getting worse.

This increase is likely a lasting after-effect of the Great Recession that began in late 2007 — a stress-filled time that caused long-term emotional damage to many Americans. It culminated in 2019/2020 with a global pandemic.

Many people psychologically affected by these events haven't been able to get the help they need, either because they can't afford it or because their condition hampers their ability to seek out treatment.

As a result, hundreds of thousands of Americans live with serious psychological distress, an umbrella term that runs from general hopelessness and nervousness all the way up to diagnosable conditions such as depression and anxiety.

The real problem is due to a lack of understanding and recognizing what is causing this stress and anxiety, then taking appropriate steps to remove or reduce these factors.

Either we need to reduce or eliminate the stress in our life for the things that are causing the most stress. Work on changing it or changing how you're responding to it if you can't eliminate it, like a job.

Because stress is not just the project you have due on Friday. It's the people around you, it's stress of nutrition, it's stressing your brain, it's inflammation, it's how you talk to yourself, how other people talk to you. That's stress. It's finances, it's problems, it's the weather, it's the red lights you hit on your way to the job you don't like…it's the whole of the environment.

That's why it seems to be unavoidable because we all tend to say "Yes" to often, overload our schedules, desire too many things and experiences, and get frustrated by the world around us. This all seems to move at a faster and faster pace, creating a vicious cycle we can't seem to escape.

It doesn't have to be this way, there are solutions to your stress, anxiety, and overwhelm and depression. Natural solutions, so you do not get caught in the "quick-fix with a pill" solution. Because over time, it's not really a solution, just a temporary band-aid.

What the medication does is either deplete neurotransmitter levels or increases them exponentially depending upon the drug, the class and all that. Then, you end up having an out-of-balance system and the "quick-fix" has become a big, long-lasting problem.

That one prescription might scale some things down for you, so you can focus more on cleaning up the other stuff and give you a breath so that you can do it. But for most people that's not what happens. They get their prescription and that's it. They don't do anything else because miraculously whether it's a placebo or not, you feel better…for a little while, until you don't anymore.

If you are ready to let go of your anxiety and depression once and for all, utilizing completely natural and healthy solutions, then keep reading.

I'm about to show you how to take advantage of a stress eradication strategy I call anxiety and depression annihilation, just kidding its the YOUR BEST BRAIN plan.

What you are about to learn has helped others eliminate their anxiety and depression, return their bodies natural physical and mental balance, and give them back a life filled with happiness and joy.

And I'm confident it can help you too.

Anxiety Disorders were only recognized in 1980 by the American Psychiatric Association. Before this recognition, people experiencing one of these disorders usually received a generic diagnosis of "stress" or "nerves." As there was no understanding of the disorders by the health professionals, very few people received effective treatment.

Recently, there has been more media on the prevalence of anxiety, panic attacks, stress and anxiety disorders. As more people become aware of the presence of anxiety disorders, there is more interest in the appropriate treatment of these disorders. Anxiety carries less stigma now as more-and-more people from all walks of life report to their health professionals for treatment.

Depression has become the leading cause of disability claims worldwide, affecting millions and leaving a significant impact on individuals, families, and workplaces. It's more than just feeling down; it can cripple your ability to function, engage, and enjoy life. The statistics are staggering—more people are missing work or unable to carry out daily activities due to depression than almost any other condition. Despite its prevalence, many still don't understand how deep its effects go. It's time to face the truth: depression isn't just about sadness; it's a mental health crisis that requires real solutions and a shift in how we approach our well-being.

With the dawn of psychoanalysis and Freud, many people turned to the therapist's couch as a solution to their experience with an Anxiety Disorder or depression. With the advent of pharmaceuticals, drugs have been prescribed heavily for people presenting with an Anxiety and Depressive Disorders.

Until recently, even I as a professional had believed this to be the best for of treatment and tried this avenue, I've been there. But, I don't anymore.

I had depression and anxiety several years ago. I was working at a job and I started realizing, "This job is causing me to have serious panic attacks and anxiety." I've included my story at the beginning of every chapter.

I made some drastic changes and know that not everybody can or is willing do that, but I wish more people could look at the thing in their life, identify it as "this is the thing that causes me the most anxiety, stress and overwhelm," and eliminate it. I was able to step out of my anxious fear to do it because that was the only way out that I saw for myself.

What if I told you there was a way to eliminate anxiety and overwhelm without ever taking a pharmaceutical drug and exposing yourself to potential addiction or long-term reliance on medicines?

YOUR BEST BRAIN doesn't rely on the SNRI's, SSRI's or benzodiazepines so commonly prescribed as the best form of treatment today. It allows you to feel comfort and calm within your world, dramatically slashing your stress, frustration, and overwhelm without ever using a chemical crutch, which can cause brain fog, or worse and can further delay your healing.

YOUR BEST BRAIN provides the tools and strategies that you've been missing. The ones that work and have been proven by hundreds of scientific studies to be, in most cases, much more effective than those medications.

Before you can take advantage of the YOUR BEST BRAIN's powerful tactics, you may have to change your perspective. Don't even think about taking another pill again, it's not working. It never has, at best it's just been masking the real reasons for your discomfort and struggle. But, that doesn't mean to quit cold turkey. It means to evaluate.

Also, there's so many things, but again, a lot of that is how you look at it. When you hit every red light on your commute and then you get so frustrated because every red light is making you stop.

Well, you could look at that as a huge frustration or you can look at that as, "Well, I guess I have 30 seconds to myself to breathe deeply and get some good oxygen to my cells, they could use it."

There's no good reason for you not to be at ease, relaxed, comfortable and stress-free. If you apply the YOUR BEST BRAIN method I'm about to share with you, or even one of the highly effective exercises, in as little as a week you can begin to feel the pressure lift and joy begin to return.

But you won't want to stop there because when you take what you are about to learn and make it part of your world and daily habits, you will live a healthier, happier, and more fulfilling life. And probably a longer one too.

1

ANXIETY, THE BIGGEST BITCH YOU WILL EVER MEET

*"Sometimes our lives have to be completely shaken up, changed, and rearranged,
to relocate us to the place we were meant to be"*
Quotes 'n Thoughts

FREEDOM! The day I made a decision to do something about my suck ass job and the anxiety riddled life was the day I actually experienced freedom! I let daily panic attacks practically destroy my life until I felt like a nub of cheese after the cheese grater of life whittled me down to nothing. I barely had the energy to do anything about it. I was slowly gaining weight which really sucked because I just lost almost 100 pounds two years before this job.

I found myself going to the doctor's office and complained about my job, my life and 'my anxiety'. I walked out of the office with an SNRI prescription, Effexor. I felt in a fog, a daze. I took the pills that night and felt dizzy and sick. I took them again the next night and felt the same way. On the third night, I didn't take them at all. Instead I made a decision that would change everything!

Alright, let's dig in. First off, I'll be honest, this is going to take a little work. Don't worry, I'm not going to leave you to figure it out on your own, this book will guide you along and when you join my online community, you will find even more resources and plenty of support.

What exactly are we talking about when we are using the word "anxious" or "anxiety." Your dictionary is going to define it as something like: a feeling of worry, nervousness, or unease, typically about an imminent event or something with an uncertain outcome. The "uncertain outcome" piece is important, because many people worry in excess over things they either have no control over or they have no idea what is going to happen in that situation.

Hands down the BEST definition I have found for anxiety comes from Urban Dictionary "<u>The biggest</u> <u>bitch you</u> will ever meet. Only thing <u>is it's</u> inside your head." Ha! If that isn't a truth bomb I don't know what is! And man oh man can I be the biggest bitch I've ever met to myself. My inner critic was on fire and there was no dowsing the flames there.

As you read through this book, my goal is to help you understand what anxiety and depression are, what causes it, and how to recognize it within yourself. And then, how to focus your perspective surrounding anxiety and realizing that you do not own the anxiety, it is not a part of you, right? Because the thoughts of anxiety are almost always based on things out of your immediate control. Meaning, I can't control what other's think of me. I can control what I think of and about myself. Learning to tame the inner bitch is what this book is all about!

What if this doesn't work for me?

This is a great question and one that I get asked often. Firstly you need to understand what the term 'work for me' means. What is it you want to get out of the book? How much work are you willing to put in to feel differently? Do you see where I'm going here? Reading a book will not change your life, you will. You must take some action, any action to make a change happen. The magic isn't within the pages of this book, it's within you.

"Anxiety coupled with panic attacks is a debilitating way to live. Once I understood the role between nutritional elements and my anxiety, I was able to eliminate my life-debilitating panic attacks." A.K.

WHAT IF…

But what if I can't afford what is recommended?

This is another question that comes up a lot. Of course the standard response is 'can you afford not to make these changes'? I want you to really think about that for a minute. Many people say they can't afford to purchase whole foods. But they will get to the checkout aisle and put a case of soda on the counter. Or, many people will invest in their unhealthy habits by purchasing cigarettes, alcohol, processed foods, soda, etc. The list can go on. Really evaluate how you invest in the lifestyle that you are currently living and figure out what you can change or live without and go from there. Do some comparison shopping too. I buy a ton of high quality food at a discount store. It saves a lot of money doing that. And finally, remember that you don't have to change everything all at once. Start with one thing and then upgrade it. Then, move on to something else. This will make the change seamless and less costly as you slowly implement new things into your life.

Let's start things off with some goal setting. What is it that you really want to get out of this book? What do you want to change or make easier? In order to get us started on the right foot. Let's learn some simple strategies that will make goal setting and goal achieving easier.

2

CHANGE IS COMING

"Everything you want is on the other side of fear."
Jack Canfield

It was if the light bulb went off in my brain! I distinctly remember the thought that I could either take the prescription for anxiety and medicate my way through life or I could do something drastic. I chose something drastic! Doing something drastic was like fighting for my life!

See, I had been to the medication rodeo before. It was only about 5 years before this that I cold turkeyed my way off an anti-depressant (which I would never advise because I thought I would die in the process, literally). I had been prescribed the anti-depressant while pregnant with my son because I had experienced post-partum depression after my daughter was born. Basically I was prescribed an antidepressant as a 'preventative' for depression. Looking back, I see how ridiculous it was to literally create a chemical imbalance with medication to prevent something. But, I was on it for about 6 years…for post-partum depression. I know what you are thinking and I *was thinking it too. I basically couldn't get off the stuff and I didn't want to do that again. I wasn't depressed anymore, I wasn't depressed in the first place actually, I just couldn't get off the medication. But that's a story for a different chapter, or better yet…a different book.. But I vehemently knew that I didn't want to go down that road again, ever!*

I have always been extremely calculated in my life decisions. I always had a plan. Being spontaneous wasn't really something that I embraced or really even knew how to do. But, this time around I felt like I had no choice in the matter. I really felt that if I didn't make a drastic decision that I would go right off the deep end.

After two days of taking SNRI (effexor) medication, all I felt was worse. I was light headed and dizzy and basically couldn't function. I threw the medication in the garbage and I told my husband that I was quitting my job, that day. I quit my sure thing, good paying, awesome benefit job with a great retirement plan that day! I went into work almost giddy! I felt my head poke out of the turtle shell for the first time in I don't know how long. I felt a rebirth! And then it hit me like a freight train….OMG…..I don't have a real plan!

Ask Yourself Three Vital Questions:

1. What do I need to accept
2. What do I need to change
3. What do I need to leave behind

Once we understand the power of answering each of these questions, then real change can happen. Let's dig a little deeper into what each of these mean because you will be seeing them again in this book.

What do I need to accept?

First let's discuss what acceptance really is. Accepting something is the acknowledgement that it either has happened or is actually happening. If you do not accept something it is like living in a place of denial and in essence a fight against reality. If you look at acceptance it really is the idea that 'things are as they should be' and no different. This is really tough sometimes because we really don't want some crappy thing to have actually happened do we? Now, don't confuse acceptance for agreement with. They are NOT the same. We can accept something and not agree with it at the same time.

This really leads into the question of how to actually accept something. First you need to think about what it is really that you want to accept. This is where it gets tricky. When we accept it is actually letting someone or something off the hook. I know! What if they shouldn't get let off the hook? Too bad, sister, they need to be let off the hook so you can get off of it too! Acceptance is a 'real deal' look at what is actually happening. For instance, not being willing to accept a partner who doesn't help you around the house will only lead you to pain. Accepting that your partner is not going to change, regardless of all of your nagging, will allow you to move forward in decision making and in a more positive mind set.

I hear all of the time these words, "I've already accepted that". Then my next question is, "why are you in so much pain then?". If you accept something you will experience neutral feelings around it. It sounds a lot easier than it is. It will take some work, but it's worth it.

What do I need to change?

For this idea I want you to point your finger directly at what is in front of you, then turn your finger inward toward yourself until the tip of your finger hits your chest. We often look at what we need to change by pointing the finger outward and most likely toward someone else. If only my husband would (fill in the blank) then I would feel better.

However, when we point the finger only at ourselves then we really need to focus on what we need to change. This change could be how we think, what we feel and what we believe, what we are eating, whether we exercise or not. Because ultimately changing ourselves is the only control that we have.

What do I need to leave behind?

This is a tougher one and often the first thing someone thinks about doing but it ends up being the last thing that is done. For instance many of the couples I see think they need to leave each other when they get to counseling. But they haven't really figured out accept and change yet. Once they figure those out and are still miserable then leaving something behind becomes the option.

I was in a fortunate spot that I could leave my job. The day that I made that decision was the day that I actually refused to accept things as they were. I refused to be miserable and I knew that I needed to change my environment so I left it behind.

I also know there are many things we can leave behind. We can end relationships that are toxic, negative and we can also leave our own negative thought patterns behind. Additionally we can leave behind our bad habits that don't encourage health.

TESTIMONIAL

That feeling of being paralyzed with doubt. Unable to move forward in fear of what will happen. We have all experienced it. Some of us live in it daily. That overwhelming belief that you are damned if you do or damned if you don't. That is the fear that cripples us from living our life to the fullest. When we worry what others will think of us more than what we think of ourselves. The alternative to that is to believe in yourself. That's what confidence is! A belief that you are capable of anything you want. That confidence comes from listening to yourself. Stopping the negative self--talk and instead living in the present and connecting to your desires. Fear of upsetting others steals our joy! Releasing fear and moving to a state of calm confidence will allow you to experience real joy and happiness.

M.P.

3

YOU ARE WHAT YOU EAT

"Tell me what you eat, and I will tell you what you are."
Jean Anthelme Brillat-Savarin

The crazy thing is that when I quit my job I had a ton a people tell me they wish I wouldn't have. I was like, what? You people drove me to this decision and now you are remorseful? Too little, too late! This gave me more fuel to keep forging on. I still had a couple weeks to go with the job notice I gave so this is when my brain decided to do some real work.

Despite my elation with giving notice, the anxiety didn't subside right away. Granted I felt such significant relief that the panic attacks on the ride home were the first go. But I still ruminated daily about people, situations and most importantly what I had just done! It was if doing the right thing for myself was also horribly wrong. I can't even tell you how many arguments I had with myself in the car…but I won every single one of them!

I submerged myself into building a private practice so my family wouldn't be entirely penniless because of 'what I did'. But…most importantly I began to pay close attention to some new things. I focused more on getting better sleep. I was eating better food and hydrating more. I was exercising again. I had a renewed sense of spirit. And I began thinking…..how can I help others feel better, naturally?

As I climbed out of my fog, I also started to really notice that my clients were becoming sicker and sicker, despite being on medication. I would see them come into session looking drawn down, flat…medicated. I started asking more questions about how they are taking care of themselves rather than talking about thinking errors and getting med adjustments. I thought to myself, if someone challenged my thinking errors in the time of panic and anxiety I would tell them to fuck off!

We can't ever forget that we have choices. We can choose our life path and we can choose alternative methods to help us heal.

Let's talk about FOOD. It's pretty important and often neglected, abused, and ignored. We hear all the time about diet and nutrition when it comes to losing weight, gaining weight, optimal physical performance, or even the lack thereof. There is an inundation of information out there right now. Do this, don't do that! All of that information only fuels worry and anxiety. So let's pull it back a little bit and start with some small things to do that will make big change.

I'm going to cut through all of the bullshit and get completely real with you. Some of this stuff you will want to try, other things you won't. The point is you need to start somewhere, so why not start right here?

 Another way to look at change is with a "good, better, best' approach. I learned this from a dear friend, Marcia and I will never forget it because it makes damn good sense.

Three categories of change:

1. Good
2. Better
3. Best
4. Some days will just be 'good enough'

When we make change we often want ALL OF THE CHANGE! But, when we fail at all of it, we actually can end up doing none of it, am I right? For example, if you want to start your day with a nutrient dense smoothie that is a great idea, but one that can be complicated (especially if you are feeling like crap) to do. So….a 'good' smoothie is something entirely pre-made (high protein, low sugar) no mess, no fuss. A 'better' smoothie is getting some protein powder, powder green and some almond milk in a shaker cup. The 'best' smoothie is getting out your high power blender and putting in all whole foods and whipping up something fierce! The goal is not perfection. The goal is doing something different, something good for you! Good, Better, Best! Depending on where you are in the process the best you can do, might just fall in the 'good' category and that can make a big difference! What I really like to do is to rack up a bunch of changes that fall into the 'good' category. We can stack good category changes together and now we are setting ourselves up for even bigger changes that might actually be in the 'best' category.

Let's Start With **THE BRAIN**

OMG, the brain! You all know I love the brain. I tell people all of the time the brain is amazing, incredible and sooo stupid at the same time. It can trick us making us think we are scared or anxious when we are really just excited! Our brain has trouble differentiating emotions such as emotional pain or physical pain. It thinks it's the same! Or fear versus excitement, it can't tell them apart. What does tell those things apart is our thoughts around them.

Our brain will engage the nervous system and then our thoughts will come into play. For instance, let's pay attention to our body for a moment. Pretend you are getting ready to give a big speech. You might have butterflies in your stomach, start to sweat a little bit and maybe fidget around. Your thoughts around that will dictate whether you decide to view this as fear or excitement, "I can't do this, it's too much for me!" versus "I'm so excited that all of these people are here to see me!". Do you get the difference? Our lizard brain doesn't get the difference until we tell it what's happening.

Our fight/flight is in place to protect us from harm. If we didn't have it our species would have probably died off a very long time ago. When we are in fight or flight we don't have the ability to make decisions, think through things or access our coping strategies. When a threat happens, our adrenalin kicks in shutting down our prefrontal cortex (thinking brain) and allows us to instinctually go! It's also when we say and do things we wish we wouldn't have said or done. But our brain doesn't care at this point because we are running away from the threat, which turned out to be a stick, not a snake. See? Our brain can be really stupid sometimes. So…we get to figure out how to slow it down so we can make better decisions even when a perceived threat arrives.

Ready for the good stuff? 'Cause here's the nitty gritty

FOOD

The food section of this book is going to be the most difficult section. Not because it is hard, but because you've likely had decades of 'diet' advice that is calling all of the shots for you. The health of your brain (and body) rely on nutrients. Every nook and cranny of your body needs fuel for you to thrive. The problem is that we constantly roll against diet culture that says all food is food and you need to be in a calorie deficit. I want you to know something about food. It is not all created equal. In fact there is a ton of research about how processed foods are not good for you. Not only do they not nourish your brain and body, but they can absolutely cause inflammation which we know is largely implicated in mental health problems.

This is how ingrained diet culture is. When I get a new client I ask what their goals are. The first goal on the list is to lose weight. Keep in mind we are talking about mental health, not weight and yet there it is. I will never tell you to lose weight, but I will tell you to eat differently. Unlike weight loss culture, this is not about calories and you won't gain weight either. This is about brain fuel. I will tell you that you can be thin or overweight and if you don't start looking at food as nourishment, you will still feel like crap.

Alright I know this might seem weird to say…but, girl….you have to eat! It is amazing to me how little we actually eat. The first

question I ask my clients is "when is the last time you ate?".
Typically the response is rather shocking. The answers vary from 1.
Not knowing 2. More than 10 hours ago 3. Not eating for an entire
day 4. Drinking coffee in the morning and soda all day. 5. Eating
high sugar or processed food of little nutrient value.

I'm not exaggerating with those responses. 99.9% of the time
people who struggle with anxiety and depression (at least the ones
that I have seen) fall into one of those five categories. Why is this
important? Two reasons, well probably more, but for now I will
stick with two.

1. The role of reactive hypoglycemia and anxiety/depression
2. Lack of brain food that supports neurotransmitters and the
    supportive role of nutrient co-factors.

I typically get some push back around food. Because we live in a
body conscious, diet culture world people are worried about gaining
weight asking people to eat is a challenge. Often times anxiety has
caused some weight loss that ends up being a 'nice' surprise.
However, how the weight was lost is typically not sustainable
anyway and has starved your brain of essential nutrients. I need you
to trust me on this one. See when we are in fight or flight our
stomach does not digest well so you might have no appetite or when
you do eat, you might have an upset stomach. So….you don't eat.

NOT EATING MAKES THE ANXIETY AND DEPRESSION WORSE!

Or, alternatively being in a depressed state has caused some weight
gain. With each pound gained you get more and more fearful of

gaining more. One of two things happen, you either emotionally eat more or you starve yourself and your brain essentially.

We now know that eating heavily processed foods has a negative relationship with your mental health. That has been heavily researched and something you absolutely cannot ignore any longer. Not all food is created equally especially when you are dealing with mental health issues.

The following are general dietary guidelines for the purpose of reducing inflammation in your body (more about inflammation later). If you have a question about a particular food, check to see if it is on the food list. Do not make substitutions except those outlined in these instructions or recommended by your medical practitioner. You should, of course, avoid any foods to which you are intolerant or allergic, even if they are listed here.

Select fresh foods whenever you can. If and when possible, choose organically grown fruits and vegetables to eliminate pesticides and chemical residue consumption. Rinse fruits and vegetables thoroughly.

If you select animal sources of protein, look for free-range or organically raised chicken, turkey or lamb. Trim visible fat and prepare by broiling, baking, stewing, grilling, or stir-frying. Cold-water fish (e.g. salmon, mackerel and halibut) is another excellent source of protein and the omega-3 essential fatty acids, which are important nutrients in this diet. Fish is used extensively. If you do not tolerate fish, talk to your healthcare practitioner about possible substitutions. He or she may suggest supplemental fish oil (only high quality).

If all of that seems overwhelming then start small and think about "Good, Better and Best" You can do this, I know you can!

REACTIVE HYPOGLYCEMIA

In layman's terms low blood sugar. No, this does not mean you are diabetic or heading toward diabetes. Typically our blood sugar rises and falls gently throughout the day. But if we don't eat, or eat sugary foods (including alcohol) our blood sugar will fall (actually nose dive). This can cause us to have little energy and have little motivation. Also when this happens our body produces adrenaline. When stressed out (and anxiety/depression can do this so can lack of food) our body prepares itself by ensuring that enough sugar or energy is readily available. Insulin levels fall, epinephrine (adrenaline) levels rise. We are now in fight and flight. Our pre-frontal cortex (thinking brain) shuts off and now we are saying and doing things we wish we wouldn't have said or done. We are also experiencing anxiety and possibly panic attacks. We can't think straight and access any tools that will help. When blood sugar is low, we are in a state of fatigue, low energy, depression.

Some typical times of day that you experience anxiety that could be linked to hypoglycemia are upon rising, around 4pm and in the middle of the night. Adrenaline doesn't give a crap if its 2am, it will jar you awake and now you are up! Some times you might experience depression as the 2pm slump or right when you get home from work. Your brain has been starved. Side note, if your spouse/partner or kiddos (or you!) come home from work or school as crabby, irritable or with raging emotions, they are most likely experiencing reactive hypoglycemia. With adults this happens typically because food is viewed as negotiable all day. Surviving on a coffee breakfast and maybe a gas station roller dog diet isn't helping anything here. For your kids its literally because their last meal was hours before and they likely don't have the ability to grab a snack on their own.

SUPER HERO NOTE: if you kiddo is a behavioral problem at school, have them write in an IEP or a 504 plan protein snack breaks. I've done this before and it make a world of difference.

How do you combat hypoglycemia? Make sure your blood sugars are stabilized. In an effort of overcorrection eat protein every 2-3 hours, reduce sugar and particularly don't eat a large meal or a sugary snack before bed. Remember the good, better and best scenario? Think of protein like that too. Keep easy to eat protein with you at all times. You don't have to have a turkey leg sticking out of your mouth all day. You can have a cheese stick, or a pre-made protein shake. If the idea of food turns you off right now, then stick a straw in a protein shake and sip on it all day.

The next question I usually get is, how many grams of protein should I be eating? Here is my response….I don't care! I know for sure that you aren't eating enough now so work on improving that. Don't stress yourself out by being 'perfect'. Improve what you are doing now. Eat enough protein that you feel good, just focus on the 3 hour window. That's your desired amount and that is 'good' enough.

FOODS to AVOID

Yes, you knew there was going to be a list of food that you should avoid. You may not like the list, but….here goes! Remember you don't have to be perfect, you just have to start somewhere.

Caffeine:

When you have anxiety or depression, caffeine is not your friend. OMG this is a tough one, I know! Asking me to pry my morning coffee out of my lifeless hands is No Bueno! But…I have had to cut it out of my life to make sure that it isn't hurting me. I know we think caffeine/coffee/energy drinks help us to stay alert. But really it might be making your fatigue worse (adrenals/cortisol) and also amping up anxiety. When you caffeine crash you make your depression worse. I'm pretty sure the purpose of this book is to help you reduce anxiety and depression. So…caffeine made the top of the list. Caffeine is a powerful STIMULANT. It can trigger fight or flight (again engaging the entire adrenaline process). It can also impair sleep. One cup of caffeine can impair sleep for 24 hours! What the living F*CK! Additionally, slugging down caffeine in the morning doesn't allow your natural awakening response to kick in. When you first start eliminating caffeine, do these 2 things. Firstly, don't drink it first thing in the morning, wait at least 2 hours after wakening for that first (and only cup). Second, know how much you are actually drinking. For instance, most people say they have only one cup a day. That cup is a 32oz mug. That's 4 cups a day or even more! OK….did I make my point? Put down the coffee mug, the soda and energy drinks. Replace it with organic decaffeinated coffee, teecino, herbal teas or maybe just a lot more water. I know, I know…it you might feel really terrible for a couple of days, but it will pass … you will survive.

Gluten:

Things just keep getting harder don't they? I said caffeine and now I'm attacking gluten. UGH! Alright, alright…I know…this is probably even tougher than caffeine. But gluten is an inflammatory food and we eat a lot of it. Gluten, from the Latin, "glue" is a composite of proteins comprised of gliadin and glutenin, found in wheat. Inflammation isn't just limited to your joints…it's also in your gut and in your brain. There was a recent study that found that almost 20% of celiac disease sufferers experience depression and anxiety. Once gluten was eliminated it lessened or subsided altogether. People who test negative for celiac but who test positive for gluten sensitivity also have higher rates of depression and anxiety. I decided to go gluten free in 2017. Now if I have eaten gluten I can tell. My symptoms emerge about 24-48 hours after the ingestion. I am fatigued beyond belief. It feels like I can't even open my eye lids. Whatever you do…don't go out and buy gluten free substitutions for everything. Those are filled with chemicals and are really expensive. Instead look for whole foods. It's not as difficult as you might think and your brain will thank you for it.

Gluten is hidden in many things. So the easiest thing to do is to eliminate the low hanging fruit first. Breads, pastas, cereals, baked goods, cereal bars, alcoholic beverages, some candy, soups, crackers, etc. A quick google search will show you what foods to look for and what to avoid.

I know earlier I said not to just exchange food for the gluten free version, but lets say you eat sandwiches for lunch or like toast now and again. Go ahead and have some gluten free bread on hand for those occasions. What I meant was not to go crazy purchasing a bunch of processed gluten free junk. Trust me its out there, its still processed and it still isn't great for you.

Dairy:

I'm absolutely torturing you aren't I? Gluten and Casein (Dairy) have great molecular similarity. We can think of them kind of like the Bonnie and Clyde to mental health problems. Dairy is inflammatory and can cause a host of digestive problems. Remember gut and brain inflammation are close cousins. Dairy is a tougher one for me because I'm in Wisconsin and everything has dairy (think cheese). But, it is worth the hassle for a while to cut dairy out to see if you react to it when you put it back in your diet.

Dairy can impact mental health for some people due to several factors. Here's a breakdown of why dairy might be problematic for mental health:

1. **Lactose Intolerance**: Many people are lactose intolerant, meaning they have difficulty digesting lactose, the sugar found in milk. This can lead to digestive issues such as bloating, gas, and diarrhea, which can indirectly affect mood and overall well-being.

2. **Casein Sensitivity**: Casein is a protein in dairy that some people have difficulty digesting.

This can cause inflammation and digestive issues, which may contribute to feelings of discomfort and stress.

3. **Hormones and Antibiotics**: Some dairy products contain traces of hormones and antibiotics used in dairy farming. These substances can potentially disrupt the body's hormonal balance, affecting mood and mental health.

4. **Inflammation**: For some people, dairy can contribute to inflammation in the body. Chronic inflammation is linked to various mental health issues, including depression and anxiety.

5. **Nutrient Imbalance**: While dairy is a good source of calcium and vitamin D, some dairy products, particularly those that are highly processed, can be high in unhealthy fats and sugars. Consuming these in excess can contribute to poor physical health, which in turn can negatively impact mental health.

6. **Gut-Brain Connection**: The gut-brain axis is a complex communication network between the gut and the brain. Dairy products can affect gut health, particularly in those who are sensitive to dairy. An imbalance in gut bacteria can lead to issues like leaky gut syndrome, which is associated with inflammation and mental health disorders.

7. **Individual Sensitivities**: Some people may have individual sensitivities or allergies to dairy that can cause physical symptoms such as headaches, fatigue, and irritability. These symptoms can, in turn, affect mental health.

It's important to note that not everyone will experience negative effects from dairy.

For many people, dairy is a nutritious part of their diet. However, if you suspect that dairy might be affecting your mental health, it might be worth trying an elimination diet to see if your symptoms improve. Always consult with a healthcare professional before making significant changes to your diet.

Sugar:

There is probably enough information floating around the internet about the problems with sugar. ADDED sugar (not sugar from fruit in its whole form) is another inflammatory food but it also causes reactive hypoglycemia. So this is a double the pleasure double the fun 'food' that has got to go!

Sugar can negatively impact mental health in several ways. Here's a breakdown of why consuming too much sugar might be bad for your mental well-being:

1. **Blood Sugar Swings**: Eating sugary foods causes rapid spikes in blood sugar levels, followed by crashes. These fluctuations can lead to mood swings, irritability, and symptoms of anxiety and depression. The body's response to these crashes can also include the release of stress hormones like adrenaline, which can exacerbate feelings of anxiety.

2. **Inflammation**: High sugar intake can lead to chronic inflammation in the body. Inflammation is linked to a variety of mental health issues, including depression and anxiety. Inflammatory processes can affect brain function and mood regulation.

3. **Gut Health**: The gut-brain axis is a critical pathway connecting your digestive system to your brain. Excessive sugar consumption can disrupt the balance of beneficial bacteria in the gut, leading to dysbiosis. This imbalance can influence mental health, contributing to issues like depression and anxiety.

4. **Nutrient Deficiency**: Diets high in sugar often lack essential nutrients because sugary foods typically provide "empty" calories with little nutritional value. A lack of important nutrients like vitamins, minerals, and omega-3 fatty acids can impair brain function and mood stability.

5. **Addiction and Cravings**: Sugar can be addictive, leading to a cycle of cravings and consumption. This cycle can have psychological effects, such as increased feelings of stress and guilt, as well as physical effects that contribute to poor mental health.

6. **Hormonal Imbalances**: Consuming too much sugar can affect the balance of hormones that regulate mood, such as insulin and cortisol. Insulin spikes from high sugar intake can lead to insulin resistance over time, which is linked to an increased risk of depression.

7. **Sleep Disruption**: High sugar intake can interfere with sleep patterns. Poor sleep is closely linked to mental health issues like anxiety and depression. A diet high in sugar can lead to trouble falling asleep and staying asleep, further impacting mental well-being.

8. **Weight Gain and Self-Esteem**: High sugar consumption is often linked to weight gain.

Struggles with weight can impact self-esteem and body image, which can contribute to feelings of depression and anxiety.

Reducing sugar intake and maintaining a balanced diet rich in whole foods, such as fruits, vegetables, lean proteins, and whole grains, can help support better mental health. If you think sugar is affecting your mental health, consider speaking with a healthcare professional for personalized advice.

For good mental health, it's best to minimize your intake of added sugars. While there's no specific amount that guarantees mental well-being, following general guidelines can help support both physical and mental health. Here are some recommendations to aim for:

1. **World Health Organization (WHO)**: Less than 10% of your total daily calorie intake from added sugars, with an ideal target of less than 5%. For an average adult, this equates to about 25 grams (6 teaspoons) of added sugar per day for optimal benefits.

Soda, Energy Drinks, Juices and Alcohol:

I put these altogether for a couple of reasons. Not only do some of them involve caffeine, but they all involve sugar and chemicals you just don't need right now. We are trying really hard to avoid that. What about sugar free drinks? Same deal! Fake sugars are inflammatory. Additionally when we fill up on these beverages we aren't eating and we are in sugar overload…what does that cause? You got it! Hypoglycemia! Now, I understand that special occasions happen or you just have a hankering for some soda sometimes. Just pay close attention to how you feel afterwards. The key is to not deprive yourself either, but if soda was a problem for you before it is best to keep your distance for quite some time until you get the hang of prioritizing your brain over anything else. Let's break it down

Soda

1. **High Sugar Content**: Sodas are packed with added sugars, leading to rapid spikes in blood sugar levels followed by crashes. These fluctuations can cause mood swings, irritability, and symptoms of anxiety and depression.
2. **Caffeine**: Many sodas contain caffeine, which can increase anxiety and disrupt sleep patterns, contributing to poor mental health.
3. **Artificial Ingredients**: Sodas often contain artificial sweeteners, colors, and preservatives that can have adverse effects on brain function and mood.

Energy Drinks

1. **Excessive Caffeine**: Energy drinks often have high levels of caffeine, which can lead to increased anxiety, nervousness, and even panic attacks. Excessive caffeine can also cause sleep disturbances, exacerbating mental health issues.
2. **High Sugar Levels**: Like soda, energy drinks are high in sugar, leading to blood sugar spikes and crashes that can affect mood and energy levels.

3. **Additives and Stimulants**: Energy drinks contain various stimulants and additives that can impact the nervous system, potentially causing jitteriness, anxiety, and heart palpitations.

Juices

1. **Hidden Sugars**: Many commercially available juices contain added sugars, even if they are marketed as healthy. High sugar intake can lead to blood sugar fluctuations, mood swings, and increased risk of anxiety and depression.
2. **Lack of Fiber**: Unlike whole fruits, juices often lack fiber, which helps regulate the absorption of sugar into the bloodstream. This can lead to rapid spikes and drops in blood sugar levels, impacting mood and mental clarity.
3. **Nutrient Imbalance**: Consuming juices instead of whole fruits can lead to a lack of essential nutrients and fiber, which are important for overall mental and physical health.

Alcohol

1. **Depressant Effects**: Alcohol is a central nervous system depressant that can exacerbate symptoms of depression and anxiety. While it might provide temporary relief, it ultimately disrupts brain chemistry and mood regulation.
2. **Sleep Disruption**: Alcohol interferes with the quality of sleep, particularly the REM sleep stage, which is essential for emotional regulation and mental health. Poor sleep can lead to increased stress, anxiety, and depression.

3. **Nutrient Depletion**: Excessive alcohol consumption can deplete the body of essential vitamins and minerals, particularly B vitamins, which are crucial for brain function and mood stability.

4. **Addictive Properties**: Alcohol can be addictive, and dependency can lead to a range of mental health issues, including increased anxiety, depression, and cognitive impairments.

Reducing the intake of soda, energy drinks, sugary juices, and alcohol can positively impact mental health by stabilizing mood, reducing anxiety, and improving sleep and overall brain function. Opting for healthier alternatives like water, herbal teas, and whole fruits can support both physical and mental well-being.

Processed and Ultra processed Foods in General

What are processed/ultra processed foods anyway? Well, processed foods are foods that have been altered from their natural state in some way, usually for convenience, shelf life, or flavor. This can include things like canned vegetables, frozen meals, or bread. They often contain added ingredients such as salt, sugar, or preservatives.

Ultra-processed foods take this a step further. They are typically made from multiple ingredients and include industrial formulations. These foods often have little to no resemblance to their original form and are designed to be tasty and convenient. Examples include sugary drinks, packaged snacks like chips or cookies, instant noodles, and many fast foods. They often contain additives, artificial flavors, and colorings.

In simple terms, while processed foods have been changed a bit for convenience, ultra-processed foods are highly manufactured products loaded with extra ingredients to make them extra tasty and long-lasting.

Research indicates that there is a significant link between the consumption of processed and ultra-processed foods and mental health issues. Here's a summary in layman's terms:

1. **Processed Foods**: While not all processed foods are bad, those high in added sugars, unhealthy fats, and sodium can contribute to mental health issues. Consuming a diet high in these foods has been associated with increased rates of depression and anxiety. The lack of essential nutrients in these foods can negatively impact brain function.

2. **Ultra-Processed Foods**: The impact is more pronounced with ultra-processed foods. Studies show that diets high in ultra-processed foods are linked to a higher risk of depression, anxiety, and other mental health problems. These foods can cause inflammation in the body, which is believed to affect brain function and mood.

3. **Nutrient Deficiency**: Ultra-processed foods are often low in the nutrients that are crucial for mental health, such as vitamins, minerals, and omega-3 fatty acids. This lack of nutrients can contribute to poor mental health.

4. **Blood Sugar Levels**: These foods can cause spikes and crashes in blood sugar levels, which can lead to mood swings and irritability. Consistent consumption can contribute to more severe mood disorders over time.

5. **Gut Health**: There's a growing body of research showing that gut health plays a significant role in mental health. Processed and ultra-processed foods can disrupt the balance of good bacteria in the gut, leading to issues that can affect the brain.

In summary, a diet high in processed and ultra-processed foods can contribute to mental health problems due to poor nutrient content, inflammation, blood sugar fluctuations, and negative impacts on gut health. Eating a balanced diet rich in whole, unprocessed foods is generally recommended for better mental well-being.

Processed and ultra-processed foods can play a big role in causing inflammation in our bodies. Here's how it works:

1. **Added Sugars and Unhealthy Fats**: Many processed and ultra-processed foods are packed with added sugars and unhealthy fats like trans fats and refined oils. These ingredients can trigger inflammation. For example, sugary snacks and sodas can cause spikes in blood sugar and insulin levels, which can lead to an inflammatory response.

2. **Preservatives and Additives**: These foods often contain various artificial preservatives and additives to extend shelf life and enhance flavor. Some of these substances can cause inflammation in the body because they're foreign chemicals that our immune system reacts to.

3. **Low Nutrient Density**: Ultra-processed foods typically lack essential nutrients like antioxidants, vitamins, and minerals that help fight inflammation.

Without these protective nutrients, your body is more prone to inflammatory responses.

4. **Gut Health Disruption**: Our gut health is crucial for managing inflammation. Processed foods can disrupt the balance of good bacteria in the gut, leading to a condition known as dysbiosis. This imbalance can cause the gut lining to become more permeable, allowing harmful substances to enter the bloodstream and trigger inflammation throughout the body.

5. **High Salt Content**: Many processed foods have high salt content, which can contribute to inflammation, particularly in the blood vessels, leading to high blood pressure and other cardiovascular issues.

Inflammation isn't always bad; it's your body's way of protecting itself. But chronic inflammation, which can be fueled by a diet high in processed and ultra-processed foods, can contribute to various health issues, including mental health problems, heart disease, diabetes, and more.

So, while those convenient snacks and quick meals are fine once in a while, it's better for your long-term health to focus on whole, unprocessed foods that naturally help keep inflammation in check.

Here's a list of some of the most common processed and ultra-processed foods:

Processed Foods

1. Canned vegetables and fruits
2. Frozen vegetables with added sauces
3. Packaged breads and buns

4. Breakfast cereals
5. Cheese food
6. Canned soups
7. Jams and jellies
8. Pickles and olives
9. Smoked meats like ham and bacon
10. Bottled sauces and salad dressings

Ultra-Processed Foods

1. Sugary drinks (sodas, energy drinks)
2. Packaged snacks (chips, pretzels)
3. Instant noodles
4. Fast food (burgers, fries, pizza)
5. Packaged cookies and pastries
6. Sweetened breakfast cereals
7. Ready-to-eat meals (microwave dinners)
8. Candy bars and chocolate
9. Processed meat products (hot dogs, sausages)
10. Ice cream and frozen desserts

These lists cover some of the most commonly found items in each category. Processed foods have undergone some level of alteration from their natural state, while ultra-processed foods are highly manufactured and often contain many added ingredients. It's important to look at labels, if you can't read it or don't know what that ingredient is…put it back on the shelf.

There are more foods that are inflammatory than what is on this list. In the spirit of change, think about what food you are willing to give up. You don't have to do all of it, start with one thing. But in order to know if you react to the food you will have to make a 30 day commitment to elimination. Giving something up a 'little bit' won't yield the results you are looking for. Again, when making changes…think Good, Better and Best. Maybe if the idea of giving up coffee freaks you out, then make a switch to organic decaf coffee. That would be a good change.

FOOD TO EAT and ENJOY!

Protein:

Protein is not only a great way to stabilize your blood sugar, but it is the building blocks of your primary neurotransmitters (we will talk about those in a minute). Organic, grass fed protein sources are the best. So if you want to go that route, have at it! But if you are in the beginning stages of this go ahead and just think about including decent quality protein, meats, eggs, nuts in your diet. If you are eating sandwich meat make sure those are nitrate free and have at it. You can also use a high quality, low sugar protein shake to help out. Right now, you might not be eating any of those things so just eating protein is going to be in the 'good' category for you.

Protein plays a crucial role in maintaining mental health due to its involvement in neurotransmitter production and brain function. Amino acids, the building blocks of protein, are essential for synthesizing neurotransmitters such as serotonin, dopamine, and norepinephrine, which regulate mood, anxiety, and cognitive function. Consuming adequate protein helps stabilize blood sugar levels, preventing mood swings and irritability often associated with hypoglycemia. Moreover, protein-rich foods support overall brain health by providing essential nutrients like iron, zinc, and B vitamins, which are vital for cognitive function and energy production. Incorporating sufficient protein into your diet can thus enhance mood, improve concentration, and reduce symptoms of anxiety and depression.

Water:

You have to get hydrated! Our body is largely water and we need to keep replenishing it. Water helps our organs to do their job, helps our body to detoxify itself and helps our brain to function well. Believe it or not, there is also a good, better, best to water. If you don't drink enough water a good scenario is to drink 2 cups of water when you brush your teeth in the morning. Then keep a water bottle with you at all times and drink it throughout the day. A best scenario is to make sure you drink filtered water. I know that can be tough depending upon where you work. I used to work in a prison and couldn't haul in my own filter or even bring in a large amount of water every day. So whenever possible drink filtered water. The rest of the time just drink water, period. How much water you ask? Well, ideally half of your body weight in ounces. Plus for every cup of caffeine another 2 cups of water. But, if you are just shooting for 'good' start drinking more than you are right now and improve from there. Aim for at least 8 cups of water a day.

Water is essential for mental health because it plays a vital role in maintaining brain function and overall well-being. Adequate hydration ensures that the brain receives sufficient oxygen and nutrients, enhancing cognitive performance and concentration. Dehydration can lead to decreased energy levels, impaired mood, and difficulty focusing, which can exacerbate feelings of anxiety and depression. Furthermore, staying hydrated helps regulate body temperature and maintain cellular homeostasis, supporting the body's stress response and reducing the physical effects of stress. Drinking enough water also aids in the removal of toxins from the body, which can positively impact mental clarity and emotional stability. By prioritizing hydration, you can support optimal brain function and improve your mental health.

Whole Fruits and Vegetables:

This is the easiest one for sure and you probably have known it for quite some time haven't you? It's time to shop the perimeter of the grocery store. You really can't go wrong there can you? If you want the 'good' case scenario frozen veggies are a good place to start. A better idea is a mixture of fresh and frozen. The best scenario is fresh. As far as fruit goes…if you are sensitive to sugars make sure that you eat fruit that isn't over ripened. There is more sugar there. Also partner a fruit with some protein to keep that blood sugar in check.

Fruits and vegetables are excellent for mental health due to their rich content of essential vitamins, minerals, antioxidants, and fiber. These nutrients support brain function and protect against oxidative stress, which can damage brain cells. Vitamins such as C, E, and the B-complex group found in fruits and vegetables help produce neurotransmitters that regulate mood and cognitive function. Additionally, antioxidants combat inflammation and free radicals, reducing the risk of mental health disorders like depression and anxiety. The fiber in fruits and vegetables promotes a healthy gut microbiome, which is closely linked to brain health and emotional well-being through the gut-brain axis. By including a variety of colorful fruits and vegetables in your diet, you can enhance your mental clarity, stabilize your mood, and support overall brain health.

Healthy Fats:

Back when I was in high school the words low fat were common. We were trained that all fat is bad fat. This how now been debunked and I will tell you because I was so conditioned to believe that all fat is bad fat, this one was tough for me. However, good fats are imperative for brain health. Our cells are covered in lipid membranes, which is fat. They are also used in hormone production among other things. Some good fats are avocados, olive oil, avocado oil, coconut oil, nuts, seeds and eggs. Fats also help with satiety. I like to use an avocado in my smoothie instead of a banana. I also like to wrap avocado slices in nitrate free turkey slices, yummy! Think of the ways you can include healthy fats in your diet.

Healthy fats are crucial for mental health due to their role in brain structure and function. The brain is composed of nearly 60% fat, and essential fatty acids, such as omega-3 and omega-6, are vital for maintaining its cell membranes and facilitating efficient communication between brain cells. Omega-3 fatty acids, found in foods like salmon, walnuts, and flaxseeds, have been shown to reduce inflammation and promote the production of neurotransmitters that regulate mood, such as serotonin and dopamine. These fats also support cognitive function, memory, and learning. Consuming healthy fats helps stabilize mood, reduce symptoms of depression and anxiety, and improve overall brain health. Including sources of healthy fats in your diet is essential for optimal mental and emotional well-being.

All of this talk about food choices leads us into the neurotransmitters of our brain. Food is essential for neurotransmitter creation, function and rejuvenation. Proteins create neurotransmitters and nutrients support them. After all, this is what it's all about anyway. Without our brain we would literally cease to exist or function. So, it really does start here. So let's take a look at our neurotransmitters.

4

PREPARE TO BE MIND BLOWN!

"The mind is the source of all suffering, and it is also the source of all happiness."
Pema Chodron

I distinctly remember feverishly searching the internet (at a time when the internet had very little information on it) about how to impact someone's mood without medication. In basic psychology we used the neurotransmitters terms of dopamine and serotonin. Primarily if you had an addiction you had a problem with dopamine. If you were depressed or anxious you had a problem with serotonin. But, there wasn't a single stitch of information that answered the question how to fix that. That's as far as it went, yup you were doomed to a life struggling with dopamine and serotonin problems. This was when my own curiosity took on a life of its own. I found articles on how neurotransmitters are made - from protein and what nutrients they needed to go from an amino acid to a neurotransmitter. I then learned about amino acid supplements and would sheepishly offer them to clients like I was passing a love note in class with my foot. Guess what, they started to help and I was hooked.

NEUROTRANSMITTERS

I was recently shocked, befuddled and angry that I learned that psychiatrists don't know how a neurotransmitter is made. I was literally sitting in a training for psychiatrists and the trainer (an MD Psychiatrist) stated that very thing. I've know for a while that mental health therapists and social workers don't typically have a clue, but I was naive to think that the professionals whose only job is to impact a neurotransmitter with medications would certainly know. But, they don't. Can you believe it? I can't.

So, let's start with the basics

Neurotransmitters are natural chemicals that regulate numerous physical and emotional processes such as mental performance, emotional state, physical energy and pain response. They play an important role with optimal mental and physical health.

Neurotransmitters are naturally occurring throughout your entire body. They are crucial to feeling better. **Neurotransmitters are made from food**. Primarily from animal proteins but they require several other nutrients to play nice in order for the brain to wake up and say ahhh! So basically, nutrition plays a huge role in brain function which then plays a huge role in anxiety.

Neurotransmitters are negatively impacted from stress, drugs, alcohol, poor diet, prescription medications and basically crappy, overstressed lifestyles.

There are many neurotransmitters throughout our body, but for anxiety we are going to focus on Serotonin, GABA, Glutamate, Dopamine, Norepinephrine, epinephrine (adrenaline).

Serotonin

Many people have heard of serotonin. As a matter of fact most medications prescribed for anxiety and depression are in the SSRI (selective serotonin reuptake inhibitor) classification. I have found that most depression and anxiety is typically not serotonin related at all. If you only target serotonin it is kind of like going to the gym and only working out your legs. You won't be balanced. Many people do not find benefit in SSRI/SNRI medication, but many people have been prescribed them for multiple years. In fact, there is some emerging research that points to long term use of SSRI/SNRIs actually depleting serotonin and other neurotransmitters. This is similar to elicit drugs depleting dopamine. This serotonin depletion leads to medication stacking and increasing dosage. Most importantly it leads to people believing that there is something wrong with them and they will never be able to be without their SSRI. This is so unfortunate, but something I see frequently. What this often leads to is a lot of unnecessary suffering. Long term use of SSRI's or SNRI's create a whole host of nasty side effects one of which is emotional numbness. I mentioned that one because its actually the desired outcome.

Serotonin is often described as the happy neurotransmitter. But it is in charge of a whole lot more than just happiness. I typically describe it as the neurotransmitter that helps us be more mood flexible and have a greater ability to bounce back when things are tough. Serotonin is impacted by weather, blue lights, nutrition and screen time.

So how do we impact serotonin? Let's take a look at the pathway itself

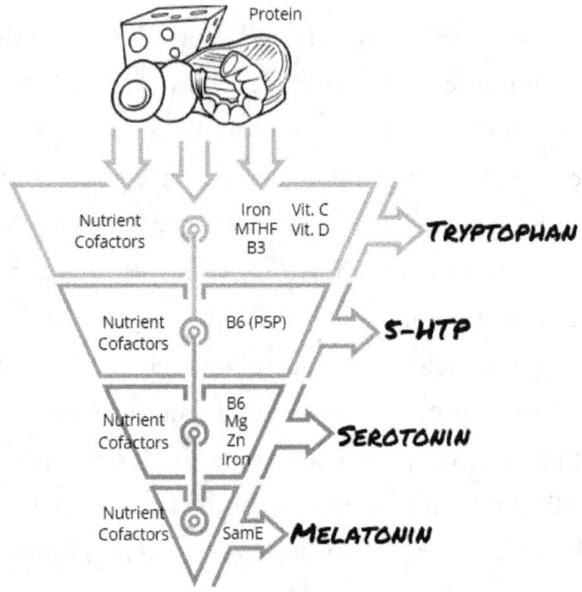

Let's take a look at how serotonin is made in the brain and how you can impact this process. Serotonin is a neurotransmitter that helps regulate mood, sleep, and even appetite. Here's a simple breakdown of the pathway that makes serotonin:

1. Starting Point: Tryptophan

The building block for serotonin is an amino acid called tryptophan. You get tryptophan from the food you eat, especially foods that are high in protein. In order for food to convert to tryptophan you will need more nutrients like Iron, methylated folate, Vitamin C, Vitamin D, B3 and enzymes

- Tryptophan-rich foods: Turkey, eggs, nuts, seeds, tofu, cheese, and salmon.

2. Conversion to 5-HTP

Once tryptophan enters your brain, it gets converted into 5-hydroxytryptophan (5-HTP). This step is facilitated by an enzyme called tryptophan hydroxylase.

- To make this process happen smoothly, vitamin B6 (found in foods like bananas, avocados, and potatoes) plays a crucial role.

3. Conversion to Serotonin

Next, 5-HTP is converted into serotonin (also known as 5-hydroxytryptamine, 5-HT). This conversion is done by an enzyme called Aromatic L-amino acid decarboxylase (AADC).

- Magnesium and zinc also play important roles in this step, helping enzymes work effectively.
- Vitamin B6 is especially important here too, as it is involved in the enzyme that converts 5-HTP into serotonin.

4. Serotonin Release

Once serotonin is made, it's stored in the nerve cells (neurons) and is released when needed to help transmit signals between nerve cells.

Dopamine/Norepinephrine/Epinephrine

This system is otherwise known as the catecholamines. It is also known as dopamine, noradrenaline and adrenaline. This is the system that I have seen the most imbalanced with clients who have depression and anxiety. Catecholamines are responsible for concentration, stress response, drive, motivation and so much more. Many people who struggle with this often complain of lethargic depression. The depression is like a pressure pulling down on the top of your head like a tight cap almost forcing your eye lids to close. It's a fatigue like no other. You might find yourself reaching for caffeine or sugar/carbs to find energy. But many are prescribed an anti-depressant for these symptoms. But an SSRI won't help it because it's a dopamine issue. Alternatively if you have high anxiety it could be due to this system as well. When your adrenaline runs high you will feel anxious and have panic attacks. There is a class of medication called SNRI (serotonin norepinephrine reuptake inhibitor) that is commonly prescribed particularly if an SSRI doesn't work. However, SNRIs are extremely difficult to get off of due to their side effects during the titration process. It will take much longer to do and you will need to be committed and diligent to supplementation and lifestyle changes. Also stimulants prescribed for ADHD impact this system tremendously. Many kids and adults who have been on stimulants for years might begin to be rageful and aggressive. They also lose weight and don't have an appetite. This is a viscous cycle because if you aren't eating you will have reactive hypoglycemia and not be fueling your neurotransmitters. It's the perfect storm of hell if you ask me.

When catecholamines are balanced you will feel motived, bright and energetic. You most likely won't need caffeine and sugar to get you going.

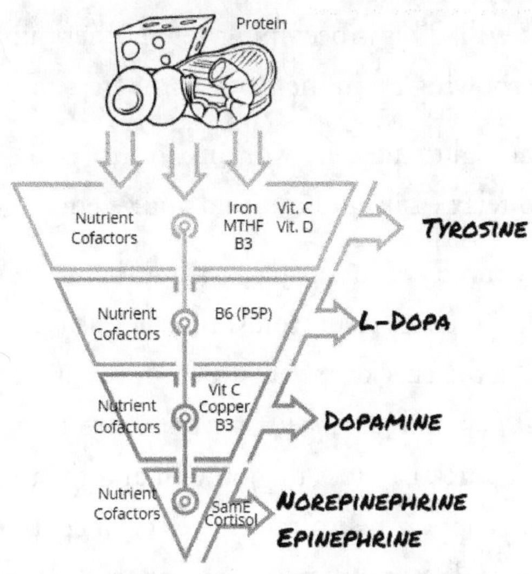

GABA

GABA has a strong relationship with glutamate. Together they are in charge of your calm. I will call them the smooth operators. When GABA is imbalanced you will likely have an inability to relax, experience panic attacks. Benzodiazepines influence GABA and are largely used to ward off panic attacks. But benzodiazepines are highly addictive. Long term use of benzos actually cause more anxiety and panic. I've seen it in my office. In extreme cases benzos cause people to be what I call 'anxiously suicidal'. Benzos are no joke and I would steer far away from them at all costs. If you are on a daily benzo please do not stop cold turkey. This could end your life! That's how deadly they are. Please seek medical attention if you want to get off of a benzo and I mean it! I typically recommend inpatient hospitalization for extreme cases. Another medication that is coming on the scene hot and heavy is gabapentin. A typical use of gabapentin was for nerve pain. Now it is being used in the mental health world as well. This is becoming yet another public health concern and is showing up in the news as the next major addiction.

When GABA and glutamate are working together you will have flow, be able to relax easily and can find your Zen!

There are many more neurotransmitters but these are key for anxiety. In order to check neurotransmitter levels I use an easy lab test. I also have some checklists that are fairly accurate to pinpoint imbalances, but pen and paper tests cannot tell you the actual level (low or high). A quick lab does the job well and then you can establish ways to support neurotransmitter balance. If you are on medication, please do not quit without support. Supporting medication use with good nutrition and supplementation in some case may actually improve the performance of your medication. Everyone is different and requires a different care plan.

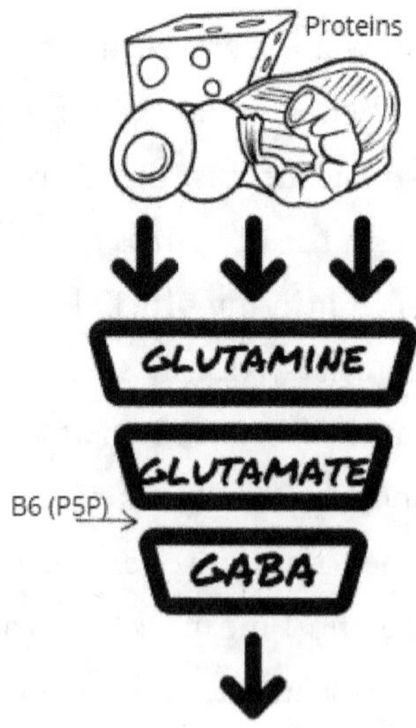

Good Mood Brain Food

For Serotonin: Think of serotonin as your "feel-good" neurotransmitter. Foods that help you make it are rich in tryptophan (like turkey, chicken, and eggs). You'll also want to eat foods with vitamin B6 (like bananas and potatoes), folate (like leafy greens and citrus), and iron (like spinach and red meat) to help turn tryptophan into serotonin.

For Dopamine: Dopamine is all about motivation and reward. To boost dopamine, you'll want to eat foods high in tyrosine (like turkey, tofu, and almonds) and support the process with zinc (found in cashews and chickpeas) and vitamin B6 (which is in foods like spinach and tuna).

For GABA: GABA is your brain's calming neurotransmitter. To make more of it, you'll need foods with magnesium (think dark chocolate, almonds, and spinach) and vitamin B6 (also found in bananas and chicken). Omega-3 fatty acids from fish like salmon and walnuts also help with GABA production.

What you eat isn't just about filling your stomach—it's about feeding your brain, too! The food you choose has a big impact on your mood because it helps produce the chemicals in your brain that control how you feel. For example, eating the right foods can boost serotonin, dopamine, and GABA—these are the neurotransmitters that keep you feeling happy, motivated, and calm. So, when you eat nutrient-rich foods, you're giving your brain the tools it needs to work its best. A balanced diet can help lift your mood, improve focus, reduce stress, and just make you feel better overall.

Simply put, the food you eat affects how you think, feel, and experience life. So, when you eat well, you're not just taking care of your body—you're taking care of your mind, too!

Nutrient	Foods to Enjoy	Supports
Protein (Amino Acids)	Turkey, chicken, eggs, fish (salmon, tuna), beans (black beans, chickpeas), lentils, tofu, quinoa, nuts (almonds, walnuts), seeds (pumpkin, sunflower)	Serotonin, Dopamine, GABA
Tryptophan (Serotonin Precursor)	Turkey, chicken, eggs, cheese, nuts (almonds, walnuts), seeds (pumpkin, sunflower), tofu, soy, fish (salmon, tuna)	Serotonin
Tyrosine (Dopamine Precursor)	Chicken, turkey, fish (salmon, tuna), soy products (tofu, tempeh), dairy (cheese, yogurt), eggs, almonds, avocados, bananas, pumpkin seeds	Dopamine
Iron	Red meat (beef, lamb), chicken, turkey, spinach, lentils, beans (kidney beans, chickpeas), tofu, quinoa, fortified cereals	Serotonin, Dopamine
Vitamin B6	Bananas, potatoes, chicken, turkey, spinach, fortified cereals, chickpeas, tuna, salmon, avocado, carrots	Serotonin, Dopamine, GABA
Vitamin B3 (Niacin)	Turkey, chicken, tuna, salmon, peanuts, whole grains (brown rice, oats), legumes (lentils, chickpeas), fortified cereals	Serotonin, Dopamine
Folate (MTHF)	Leafy greens (spinach, kale, Swiss chard), avocados, citrus fruits (oranges, lemons), asparagus, beans (black beans, lentils), fortified cereals	Serotonin, Dopamine
Vitamin C	Citrus fruits (oranges, grapefruits), strawberries, bell peppers (especially red), broccoli, Brussels sprouts, kiwi	Serotonin, Dopamine, GABA
Vitamin D	Fatty fish (salmon, mackerel, sardines), egg yolks, fortified dairy, fortified plant-based milks (soy, almond), mushrooms (exposed to sunlight)	Serotonin, Dopamine, GABA
Magnesium	Dark chocolate, almonds, spinach, avocado, pumpkin seeds, bananas, cashews, black beans, tofu	GABA
Zinc	Pumpkin seeds, cashews, chickpeas, lentils, oysters, beef, chicken, spinach, nuts (almonds, walnuts), beans	Dopamine, GABA
Copper	Shellfish (oysters, lobster), nuts (cashews, almonds), seeds (sunflower, sesame), whole grains, dark chocolate	Dopamine
Omega-3 Fatty Acids	Fatty fish (salmon, mackerel, sardines), walnuts, chia seeds, flaxseeds, hemp seeds, soybeans	Serotonin, Dopamine, GABA

SYMPTOM CHECKLIST

Here is a quick checklist to see what imbalanced neurotransmitters you might have. Rate each symptom 0-10. Ten is the worst or the most frequently felt. Give it a try. This amino acid checklist is derived from The Mood Cure by Julia Ross and adapted by the Alliance for Addiction and Mental Health Solutions.

Serotonin:

If you experience the following symptoms you may have a serotonin Imbalance

_____afternoon or evening cravings for specific food/substances

_____ negativity, depression

_____ worry, anxiety

_____ low self-esteem

_____ obsessive thought or behaviors

_____ controlling (feeling like you need to be in control)

_____ perfectionism

_____ winter blues

_____ irritability, rage (PMS)

_____ dislike hot weather

_____ panic attacks or phobias

_____ diagnosed with fibromyalgia

_____ TMJ (jaw pain)

_____ other chronic pain

_____ suicidal thoughts

_____ night-owl, hard to get to sleep

_____ insomnia, disturbed sleep

GABA

If you experience the following symptoms you might have a GABA imbalance

_____ crave carbs, alcohol or drugs for relaxation

_____ stressed and burned out

_____ unable to relax/ loosen up

_____ stiff or tense muscles

_____ often feel easily overwhelmed

_____trouble shutting brain off at night If you experience the following symptoms it might be a blood sugar/Hypoglycemia issue

_____ cravings for sugar, starch, or alcohol

_____ irritable, shaky, headachy—Especially if too long between meals

_____Anxiety upon waking, around 4pm

_____Waking unexpectedly in the middle of the night or around 2am

Dopamine

If you experience the following symptoms you might have a dopamine/epinephrine imbalance

_____ Cravings for stimulation from sugar, chocolate, caffeine, cocaine, meth

_____ depression, apathy

_____ lack of energy

_____ lack of drive

_____ lack of focus, concentration

_____ ADHD, hyperactivity

_____Leg Bouncing/fidgeter

_____Always in motion

Alright, so now you've found out what foods to eat, what neurotransmitters are and what imbalances you might have. Now what? Well, now it's time to fix those. Let's get started by learning about amino acids.

*Note: I prefer supplements that are liposomal, chewable, lozenge, liquid based. The reason for this is the absorption ability. If possible finding those kinds of supplements will improve absorption and therefore improve outcomes. Whenever possible bypassing the gut is a good idea (that's a whole different chapter). You can use capsules but if you can get your hands on other distribution methods that is optimum.

TESTIMONIAL

My daughter struggled with an excess of energy for a few years. She turned 17 this Summer and she and I decided we needed her excess energy symptoms under control before she left for college next Fall. We had Dr. Teralyn consult with us and she recommended my daughter participate in her brain health testing. The results were validating and unfortunately not great. We learned that my 17 year old's cortisol levels were very high and that her cortisol production did not follow the natural body protocol. Instead of starting highest in the morning and gradually going down throughout the day, hers spiked at night. Thus, when her brain and body should have been shutting down for sleep, she suddenly got a surge of stress hormone that took her in the opposite direction entirely.

Dr. Teralyn recommended some specific supplements and lifestyle changes to address the issues identified. She also realized that because of my daughter's age, she wanted to introduce supplements and lifestyle changes at a rate that would stick. Therefore, we started with only two supplements and one request, no blue screen after 9:00 at night.

Within two months we could see a quantifiable improvement and Dr. Teralyn added another supplement and a couple of additional lifestyle recommendations. At that same time school started so that posed some new challenges. My daughter reported that doing homework had become completely different than the year before. She said she used to sit down to start things and not be able to begin. Many times she would just stare at the computer screen or book page and not be able to start. This year she reports having no difficulty "jumping right in" to her homework. On the home side of things, my family and I have noticed a significant change in her ability to sit and have conversation normally. She used to be able to clear a room in ten minutes because her energy level was so high that she could not be calm at all. Now, she can participate in dinner conversation appropriately, sit in the living room with all of us and watch TV, and is just easier to be around. I am extremely grateful to Dr. Teralyn for her help!

D.P.

AMINO ACID Supplements (always check with your doctor or pharmacist for unintended interactions between amino acids and medications)

Many people recognize amino acids because you can find them on local health food store shelves. Many body builders have been using amino acids to build muscle forever. But, there are other benefits to using amino acids and that includes mental health and addictions. If you try any amino acids, ask your doctor or pharmacist if there are contraindications first. Also make sure that you have some vitamin C handy. If you have a reaction you can take 2000mg of vitamin C as the antidote. If you experience a negative symptom discontinue. If it is severe then get yourself to the ER. But…I don't want to scare you either. Amino acids are generally referred to as safe. But there are some contraindications so be careful like you would with anything else. You can regard amino acids as medical food as they are derived primarily from proteins.

GABA

Gamma-aminobutyric acid (GABA) is a crucial amino acid that acts as a primary inhibitory neurotransmitter in the brain, playing a vital role in regulating nervous system activity. GABA helps to reduce neuronal excitability, which promotes relaxation, reduces stress, and contributes to a sense of calmness. By inhibiting overactive brain signals, GABA can help manage anxiety, improve sleep quality, and enhance overall mental stability. Many natural supplements and foods, such as fermented foods like kimchi and certain teas, can help boost GABA levels. An adequate supply of GABA is essential for maintaining a balanced mood, reducing symptoms of anxiety, and supporting cognitive function, making it a key player in mental health.

GABA is used to augment the neurotransmitter GABA (gamma amino butyric acid), the anti-stress chemical. I prefer GABA chewables. How do you know how much to take? Well, first start with the recommended dose on the back of the bottle. Rate your anxiety from 1-5 five being the worst. Wait 15 minutes and see if there is an improvement (rate it again). If no improve take another one and wait another 15 minutes. Continue to do this until you have the desired result no more than 500mg though. It's really that easy!

Taurine

Taurine is an essential amino acid that plays a significant role in maintaining mental health and overall well-being. It is known for its calming effect on the nervous system, as it helps regulate neurotransmitter activity and stabilize cell membranes. Taurine supports the production of GABA, an inhibitory neurotransmitter that reduces anxiety and promotes relaxation. Additionally, taurine has antioxidant properties that protect the brain from oxidative stress and inflammation, which can contribute to mental health disorders. Found in foods such as meat, fish, and dairy, as well as available in supplement form, taurine is essential for cognitive function, mood regulation, and stress reduction. By ensuring adequate taurine intake, you can support a balanced mood, enhance mental clarity, and improve overall brain health.

Taurine is another relaxing amino acid, similar in structure and effect to GABA. Many people think taurine is a stimulant because it is used in so-called 'energy drinks', but it is not. It helps you relax and unwind from high levels of adrenalin, much like GABA.

L-Glutamine

Glutamine is a conditionally essential amino acid that plays several crucial roles in supporting mental health and overall well-being. As the most abundant amino acid in the body, glutamine serves as a primary fuel for intestinal cells, supporting gut health and integrity. This is significant because a healthy gut is closely linked to improved mood and cognitive function through the gut-brain axis. Glutamine also helps maintain optimal brain function by promoting neurotransmitter synthesis, including glutamate and GABA, which are essential for brain communication and mood regulation. Additionally, glutamine supports immune function, reduces inflammation, and helps protect against oxidative stress, all of which are important factors in maintaining mental health. Foods rich in glutamine include protein-rich sources like meat, fish, dairy, and legumes. Supplementing with glutamine may be beneficial for individuals looking to support their mental clarity, emotional balance, and overall brain health.

L-Glutamine is a perfect fuel for the whole brain, balancing blood sugar levels to maintain energy and clear thinking. Glutamine is also good to help with gut health. Blood sugar deficiency symptoms: irritability, shakiness, weakness, dizziness, especially if too many hours have passed since the previous meal. Glutamine is great to have on hand (put it in a smoothie too) to stabilize blood sugar. You can also use it bedside if you wake up in the middle of the night, it might help you get back to sleep.

NOTE: Be cautious about taking L-glutamine if you have manic depression (bipolar disorder). While low doses of L-glutamine may relieve bipolar depression, in approximately 50% of bipolar cases normal doses of L-glutamine can trigger mania.

SAMe

S-adenosyl-L-methionine (SAMe) is a naturally occurring compound in the body that plays a crucial role in supporting mental health and overall well-being. SAMe is involved in the methylation process, which is essential for the synthesis of neurotransmitters like serotonin, dopamine, and norepinephrine. These neurotransmitters play key roles in regulating mood, emotions, and cognitive function. SAMe also contributes to the production of phospholipids, which are crucial for maintaining cell membrane integrity in brain cells. Supplementing with SAMe has been studied for its potential to improve symptoms of depression, enhance mood stability, and alleviate anxiety. Additionally, SAMe has anti-inflammatory properties and helps support liver health, which can indirectly benefit mental health by reducing systemic inflammation and supporting detoxification processes. SAMe is naturally found in small amounts in foods like meat, fish, and dairy, and is also available as a dietary supplement. Incorporating SAMe into your diet or supplement regimen may help support mental clarity, emotional well-being, and overall brain health.

SAMe is involved with the production of several other brain neurotransmitters, dopamine and norepinephrine. Maintaining adequate levels of these foundational neurotransmitters is essential in supporting feelings of well-being. Recent controlled trials have demonstrated the efficacy of SAMe promoting a happy, balanced mood. SAMe is a tricky one for me. If you have high anxiety a low dose for a short period works well. I have seen anxiety increase with SAMe. So use it with caution.

L-THEANINE

L-Theanine is an amino acid primarily found in tea leaves, particularly green tea, known for its calming and relaxing effects on the mind and body. It promotes relaxation without causing drowsiness by increasing alpha brain waves, which are associated with a state of wakeful relaxation and enhanced mental clarity. L-Theanine also stimulates the production of neurotransmitters such as dopamine, serotonin, and GABA, which play crucial roles in mood regulation, stress response, and cognitive function. By modulating these neurotransmitters, L-Theanine helps promote a sense of calmness, reduce anxiety and stress, and improve focus and concentration. It is often used to enhance cognitive performance and support mental health, particularly in managing symptoms of anxiety and enhancing overall relaxation without sedation. L-Theanine supplements are available and can be beneficial for individuals seeking natural ways to support their mental clarity, emotional well-being, and stress management.

L-Theanine is an amino acid that is not common in the diet (not one of the essential amino acids or even one of the common nonessential amino acids). L-Theanine has structural similarity to glutamine and both neurotransmitters that are produced from it (GABA and glutamate) and is known to reach the brain and act in the brain following oral ingestion. L-Theanine helps to 'modulate' neurotransmitters bringing them into balance much like an adaptogenic herb.

The properties of L-theanine can be summed up as being a relaxing agent without sedation (relative to something like lemon balm which relaxes but may also sedate), and is also implicated in reducing the perception of stress and slightly improving attention. While L-theanine does not appear to induce sleep, it is generally helpful in helping relax before bedtime.

Interestingly, the relaxing and attention promoting properties of L-theanine coupled with the lack of sedation may L-Theanine have its most significant supplemental role in attenuating the 'edge' of many stimulants. A combination of L-Theanine with caffeine (200mg each) is noted to be synergistic in promoting cognition and attention.

I love theanine. I view it as an all around 'good guy' and a real 'team player'. If you try nothing else, give theanine a trial and see if you like it.

5HTP

5-Hydroxytryptophan (5-HTP) is a naturally occurring amino acid and chemical precursor to serotonin, a neurotransmitter that regulates mood, sleep, and appetite. 5-HTP is produced from the amino acid tryptophan in the body and is essential for the synthesis of serotonin. Serotonin plays a crucial role in mood regulation, promoting feelings of happiness and well-being. By increasing serotonin levels in the brain, 5-HTP may help alleviate symptoms of depression, anxiety, and insomnia. It is also believed to have a positive effect on appetite control and weight management. 5-HTP supplements are commonly used to support mental health, improve mood, and enhance overall well-being. However, it is important to use 5-HTP supplements under the guidance of a healthcare professional to ensure proper dosage and safety, as excessive serotonin levels can lead to adverse effects. Incorporating 5-HTP into your wellness regimen may help support emotional balance, improve sleep quality, and promote a positive outlook on life.

The effects of 5-HTP on symptoms of depression have been well studied.

While the exact cause of depression is largely unknown, some researchers believe that a serotonin imbalance may influence your mood in a way that leads to depression.

5-HTP supplements are thought to treat depression by increasing serotonin levels.

In fact, several small studies have found that 5-HTP reduced symptoms of depression. However, two of them did not use placebos for comparison, limiting the strength of their findings.

5-HTP supplements increase serotonin levels in your body, which may improve symptoms of depression, especially when used in combination with other antidepressant substances or medications. Nonetheless, more research is needed.

If you are taking an SSRI or an SNRI either don't use 5HTP or use it under supervision. There is a risk of serotonin syndrome that cannot be ignored.

DLPA

DL-phenylalanine (DLPA) is a combination of the natural amino acid phenylalanine. It exists in two forms: D-phenylalanine, which is a synthetic form, and L-phenylalanine, which is naturally occurring and found in protein-rich foods like meat, fish, eggs, and dairy. DLPA works by supporting the production of neurotransmitters in the brain, including dopamine, norepinephrine, and epinephrine, which are essential for regulating mood, motivation, and stress response. By increasing levels of these neurotransmitters, DLPA may help improve mood, reduce feelings of pain and discomfort, and enhance mental alertness and focus. DLPA is often used as a dietary supplement to support mental health, alleviate symptoms of depression and anxiety, and enhance overall cognitive function. It is important to consult with a healthcare provider before starting DLPA supplementation, especially if you have a medical condition or are taking medications, to ensure safety and effectiveness. Incorporating DLPA into your daily routine may contribute to better emotional well-being, increased energy levels, and improved mental clarity.

D-Phenylalanine (fee nil al a neen) extends the life of pain-relieving chemicals called endorphins. (L-phenylalanine is a form that stimulates the nervous system). D-phenylalanine is a powerful pain reliever without being a stimulant. It is available online. Most health food stores sell a mixed form called DL-Phenylalanine. Symptoms of Endorphin deficiency may include: crying easily even over commercials on television, chronic pain, emotional fragility, particularly sensitive to pain. *Use of Prescribed pain relievers like Vicodin.* Symptoms of deficiency may also include *cravings for: Numbing foods like sweets and starches, uses substances like nicotine, marijuana, heroin, or alcohol to numb feelings.*

NOTE: Don't take D- or DL-Phenylalanine if you have melanoma, Grave's disease, or phenylketonuria (PKU). Be cautious about taking Phenylalanine if you have migraines, Hashimoto's thyroiditis, high blood pressure, or manic depression (bipolar disorder).

L-Tyrosine

L-Tyrosine is a non-essential amino acid that plays a crucial role in the production of several important neurotransmitters, including dopamine, norepinephrine, and epinephrine. These neurotransmitters are involved in regulating mood, stress response, and cognitive function. Tyrosine is synthesized from phenylalanine in the body and is found in protein-rich foods such as meat, fish, dairy, nuts, and seeds.

Supplementing with L-tyrosine may support mental health by increasing the production of these neurotransmitters, which can help improve mood, enhance concentration, and promote feelings of alertness and motivation. L-Tyrosine is often used to support cognitive performance during stressful situations, such as intense physical activity or mental stress, by replenishing neurotransmitter levels depleted by stress.

Research suggests that L-tyrosine supplementation may also be beneficial for individuals experiencing symptoms of depression, fatigue, or attention deficit disorder (ADD/ADHD). It is important to consult with a healthcare provider before starting L-tyrosine supplementation, especially if you have a medical condition or are taking medications, to ensure safety and effectiveness. By incorporating L-tyrosine into your diet or supplement regimen, you may support overall mental well-being, cognitive function, and emotional resilience.

L-Tyrosine (tie row seen) is used to manufacture catecholamines (cat a coal a meens) like dopamine, norepinephrine and epinephrine. These neurotransmitters cause us to wake up in the morning alert and refreshed with a clear mind, able to concentrate and focus on our goals. Symptoms of Catecholamine deficiency may include: fatigue, unfocused, lack of motivation, depression, apathy, feeling of boredom but no energy to do anything more interesting, possibly diagnosed as "attention deficit disorder" (ADD). You can achieve your desired dose by taking the amount suggested on the back of the bottle and wait 15 minutes. Do you eyelids still feel like closing? Are you still yawing? If yes, take another one and wait 15 minutes. Keep doing this until you fatigue subsides (don't take more than 2000mg at a time). If you begin to feel jittery then your desired dose is one capsule less. You can also take 2000mg of vitamin C as an antidote to cut the impact.

NOTE: Don't take L-tyrosine if you have had melanoma, Grave's Disease, or phenylketonuria (PKU). Be cautious about taking L-tyrosine if you have migraines, Hashimoto's Thyroiditis, high blood pressure, or manic depression (bipolar disorder).

NUTRIENT CO-FACTORS

A nutrient co-factor can be described as non-protein chemical compound or metallic ion that is required for an enzyme's activity. Basically it is vitamins and minerals that are needed in order for amino acids to metabolize into neurotransmitters. Again when we go back to our conversations about nutrition now you can see that protein, vitamins and minerals are super important. In a perfect world eating a well-balanced diet should suffice. However, we are not perfect and our diets could use a good overhaul for sure. You most likely wouldn't be reading this book if you had an optimal diet anyway. Therefore high quality supplementation is needed especially for those nutrient co-factors.

Ready? Here we go! There are some simple micronutrient lab tests that will help you to really know if you are micronutrient deficient. Also keep in mind that supplementation is also dependent upon how nutrient rich your diet is. Also keep in mind that there are different forms of iron, magnesium, b vitamins etc.

TESTIMONIAL

After working with Dr. Teralyn, I honestly feel like a new person. I had been in a funk for what felt like forever—low energy, moody, just not myself. Dr. Teralyn really helped me understand how important my vitamin D levels were and how much my diet was impacting my mood.

T.P.

Alright, so we've established nutrition and helping our neurotransmitters to function properly is damn important when it comes to reducing our anxiety and improving our brain's happiness.

And you're going to tell me that organic and real food, unprocessed food without additives and preservatives and shit, is going to be too expensive and you can't do it. Well….I'm here to tell you that small changes add up and to remember our 'good, better, best' scenario.. Start somewhere, anywhere and get going! Don't let those negative thoughts about failing or not doing it right creep in there.

5

TRUST YOUR GUT

"Truth is when your mind and your gut agree."
Shannon Hale

I t's like a *PUNCH TO THE GUT! My stomach hurt so bad! For as long as I can remember I've had problems with my stomach. I remember as a kid literally passing out from intestinal pain in the middle of the night. My mom was so scared. As an adult every time I was under stress my intestines would let me know immediately, you get the drift. My poor husband can tell EVERY TIME when I'm under stress. He would just give me the 'look' and we would chuckle and then I would literally run to the bathroom and 'unload' the stress.*

Quitting my job was no different. My stomach was in absolute knots. I wasn't digesting food, it was just moving right through me. I knew this had to do with my nervous system. When you are living in your anxiety 'lizard' brain there is no time to digest food, there is only time to survive.

Have you ever felt butterflies in your stomach? Or had a pit in your stomach so big that it hurt? Have you been diagnosed with IBS,

GERD, acid reflux, etc.? This is the gut brain connection. Most people aren't just struggling with gut related issues, they are typically also struggling with mental health issues. The connection is real and it is strong.

It all starts with what you put in your mouth. Digestion of whatever you eat begins immediately upon the first chew, the first taste, the first gulp. When we are stressed out we tend to turn to comfort foods, alcohol, sugar, dairy, gluten. My favorite comfort foods are pizza and ice cream. Both things, I know now, wreak havoc on my intestinal system. Now, particularly when I eat gluten, I will feel the effects about a day or so later. Either my stomach will feel bloated and sick or I will be extremely tired and literally not be able to function the brain fog is so bad. So, I have chosen to eliminate gluten and dairy from my life. Dairy was probably harder for me than gluten because I really enjoy frozen yogurt and ice cream. I am also in Wisconsin so dairy is everywhere!

I know some people who say they don't have stomach issues. But then belch or complain about their stomach. If that happens to you..you have stomach issues! Also if you drink alcohol, eat processed foods and take prescription medication (pretty much for anything) you have stomach issues, or digestion problems. We tend to chase these issues from the time we are infants (gas drops and infant constipation) through adulthood popping antacids and then taking proton pump inhibitors (PPIs).

A lot of times our kids will complain of tummy aches, this is a first sign that they might be struggling with anxiety. They also might have eating issues, picky eaters, eat like a bird, store food in their cheeks, etc. If this is your kid, I encourage you to look at diet and work on creating a healthy microbiome.

If you struggle with irritable bowel, colitis, celiac, crohns disease then you absolutely have to focus on your microbiome. Typically people who I have seen that struggle with disease of the digestive system struggle really hard with mental health issues as well. This is primarily because of a poor diet or being in a state of denial that diet and a healthy microbiome could help them tremendously.

Ask yourself….Do you take proton pump inhibitors or PPI's? Do you have irritable bowel? How about antacids, do you take those on a regular basis? Have you ever been on antibiotics? Do people around you complain about your gas? Do you have trouble with pooping? Do you poop a lot or not enough? If any of this applies to you then you must begin to focus on improving your gut health. Most importantly, do you have mood issues despite a very healthy diet - you probably aren't absorbing nutrients so yes, you have gut problems.

FOODS to AVOID

I know, I know I'm doing it again aren't I? Here is the list of foods to eliminate and yes it's the EXACT same as the foods to eliminate to improve mental health. But in case you are reading this chapter first or cannot remember, here it is!

Caffeine:

When you have anxiety, caffeine is not your friend. OMG this is a tough one, I know! Asking me to pry my morning coffee out of my lifeless hands is No Bueno! But…I have had to cut it out of my life to make sure that it isn't hurting me. I know we think caffeine/coffee/energy drinks help us to stay alert. But really it might be making your fatigue worse (adrenal fatigue) and also amping up anxiety. I'm pretty sure the purpose of this book is to help you reduce anxiety. So…caffeine made the top of the list. Caffeine is a powerful STIMULANT. It can trigger fight or flight (again engaging the entire adrenaline process). It can also impair sleep. One cup of caffeine can impair sleep for 24 hours! What the living F*CK! OK….did I make my point? Put down the coffee mug, the soda and energy drinks. Replace it with teecino, herbal teas or maybe just a lot more water. I know, I know…it you might feel really terrible for a couple of days, but it will pass and you will survive.

Gluten:

Things just keep getting harder don't they? I said caffeine and now I'm attacking gluten. UGH! Alright, alright…I know…this is probably even tougher than caffeine. But gluten is an inflammatory food and we eat a lot of it. Gluten, from the Latin, "glue" is a composite of proteins comprised of gliadin and gluten, found in wheat. Inflammation isn't just limited to your joints…it's also in your gut and in your brain. There was a recent study that found that almost 20% of celiac disease sufferers experience depression and anxiety. Once gluten was eliminated it lessened or subsided altogether. People who test negative for celiac but who test positive for gluten sensitivity also have higher rates of depression and anxiety.

I decided to go gluten free in 2017. Now if I have eaten gluten I can tell. My symptoms emerge about 24-48 hours after the ingestion. I am fatigued beyond belief. It feels like I can't even open my eye lids. So your reaction is most likely not going to be immediate if you have a sensitivity rather than an allergy. So, pay attention to your body.

Whatever you do…don't go out and buy gluten free substitutions for everything. Those are filled with chemicals and are really expensive. Instead look for whole foods. It's not as difficult as you might think and your brain will thank you for it.

Dairy:

I'm absolutely torturing you aren't I? Gluten and Casein (Dairy) have great molecular similarity. We can think of them kind of like the Bonnie and Clyde to Anxiety. Dairy is inflammatory and can cause a host of digestive problems. Remember gut and brain inflammation are close cousins. Dairy is a tougher one for me because I'm in Wisconsin and everything has dairy (think cheese). But, it is worth the hassle for a while to cut dairy out to see if you react to it when you put it back in your diet.

Sugar:

There is probably enough information floating around the internet about the problems with sugar. Sugar is another inflammatory food but it also causes reactive hypoglycemia. So this is a double the pleasure double the fun 'food' that has got to go!

Soda, Energy Drinks, Juices and Alcohol:

I put these altogether for a couple of reasons. Not only do some of them involve caffeine, but they all involve sugar and result in reactive hypoglycemia. We are trying really hard to avoid that. What about sugar free drinks? Same deal! Fake sugars are inflammatory. Additionally when we fill up on these beverages we aren't eating and we are in sugar overload…what does that cause? You got it! Hypoglycemia!

There are more foods that are inflammatory than what is on this list. In the spirit of change, think about what food you are willing to give up. You don't have to do all of it, start with one thing. But in order to know if you react to the food you will have to make a 30 day commitment to elimination. Giving something up a 'little bit' won't yield the results you are looking for. Again, when making changes…think Good, Better and Best. Maybe if the idea of giving up coffee freaks you out, then make a switch to organic decaf coffee. That would be a good change. I have an anti-inflammatory food list in the private Facebook group that you can snag as soon as you join!

FOODS that can ENCOURAGE GUT HEALTH

There are several foods that encourage a healthy gut microbiome. They fall into two major categories, probiotics and prebiotics.

Probiotics are live bacteria and yeasts that live in your gut that are good for you. They are essentially good gut bugs. They help balance your good and bad bacteria in your gut. They are good soldiers for your microbiome. But they are fragile and can be easily wiped out by antibiotic use, poor nutrition and even stress. So it's really important to feed them well.

Prebiotics are typically high fiber foods that influence our microflora. Prebiotics are used as food for probiotics. They also help with inflammation, metabolism, weight loss, immune function and much more. So they work together with probiotics to create a healthy microbiome and a healthier you .

PREBIOTIC FOODS

- Dandelion Greens
- Garlic
- Asparagus
- Leeks
- Bananas
- Artichoke
- Apples
- Onions

PROBIOTIC FOODS

- Yogurt
- Kefir
- Sauerkraut
- Kimchi
- Miso
- Kombucha
- Pickles

PROBIOTIC and PREBIOTIC SUPPLEMENTATION

Stand in front of a shelf full of probiotics and you will quickly be over whelmed. Most likely what you will do is find the cheapest one, because you don't know what else to do! Not only that, but a lot of probiotics on the shelf are often no good, because they might not be shelf stable. So, you might just be wasting your money on something that isn't even worth it.

Because there are many strains of probiotics (think lactobacillus) it is important to find a few different reputable brands. I typically have clients purchase a different brand after every bottle has emptied. That way you are constantly feeding your microbiome different strains of probiotics. I typically do not recommend purchasing any supplements at your local big box retailer. Instead go to a mom and pop health food store and ask them for recommendations. You will be looking for a brand that is shelf stable. There are also some brands that now include prebiotics and probiotics which is win, win! My favorite probiotics are listed in the files section of my private Facebook group.

I'm going back to our good, better and best conversation from previous chapters. A good idea is to get your hands on a really good probiotic. A better idea is to begin to eliminate the inflammatory foods from your diet. The best idea is to tackle it with food and supplementation support.

One final note… alcohol has got to go, at least for a while. I want you to quit drinking wine and any other alcohol for four weeks at a minimum while we reset your gut. Alcohol is killing the good guys and helping the bad dudes to proliferate.

TESTIMONIAL

The vagus nerve is a direct connection from our gut to our brain! Our microbiome talks to our brain so many times throughout the day. If we have a healthy microbiome then amazing messages will be sent to the brain. If the microbiome is in distress and not in a healthy state, the messages to the brain will be distorted and not correctly received

R.B.

DIGESTIVE ENZYMES

Breaking down your food for digestion actually begins in your mouth. But if your stomach has too much acid or too little the digestion in your stomach will be impaired. If your stomach isn't breaking down food for full absorption then you can experience a whole host of problems. You might need some digestive enzymes if you have bloating, burping, farting, upset stomach or take a PPI or heartburn medication.

To improve digestion and therefore improve nutrient absorption a high quality digestive enzyme might just be a good idea. Digestive enzymes are essential. They turn our food into smaller compounds which include amino acids (remember the chapter on brain health here).

BETAINE HCL

Hydrochloric acid helps increase stomach acid naturally. Betaine HCL is great for chronic heartburn and indigestion. HCL taken with meals can help bring indigestion relief, improve digestion and help with absorption of essential nutrients.

ZINC

Zinc is essential for the production of hydrochloric acid in the stomach. It is a key component of the enzyme **carbonic anhydrase**, which is involved in the process of producing stomach acid. Without enough zinc, your stomach might struggle to produce adequate acid, leading to digestive problems.

When combined, **zinc and betaine HCL** work together to support optimal stomach acid production. Betaine HCL can help supply the acid directly, while zinc ensures your body has the resources it needs to produce and maintain healthy levels of stomach acid. This combination can help improve digestion and nutrient absorption, particularly for people with low stomach acid levels.

6

WHAT HAPPENED IN VAGUS DOESN'T HAVE TO STAY IN VAGUS

*"Life is like an elevator: On your way up, sometimes,
you have to stop and let some people off"*
hplyrikz.com

YOU ARE NOT GOOD ENOUGH, smart enough, pretty enough….you are just not enough! This is the godforsaken mantra that ran my life and kept me back for a very long time. The first time I remember this was in middle school solo ensemble. I was so nervous and had myself convinced that I wasn't good enough to play 'the entertainer' on my flute that I bombed the whole thing. I stood in front of the judge, my throat closed up and not a single note came out. Worse yet, the judge gave me a first place and said, "I knew you could do it". OH GREAT! Now I just earned myself the 'pity' award of 'you really aren't good enough'.

Do you know why I got a PhD? To prove to myself that I am good enough. This was so stupid! I literally got every license that I was eligible for in my state and didn't just go for the certificates I went for the master level certifications to prove my worth. What that really caused was a ton of self doubt and a lot of debt.

I will never forget one of the last straws that I had while working in that terrible job. I had a meeting with another supervisor (of all things). I'm pretty sure that this person made it their mission to break me. All of their insecurities were projected all over me like vomit that I had to fling off of me every damn day.

Anyway I had just completed my PhD and instead of remaining silent or congratulating me they decided to come into my office, shut the door and berate me. I went to my supervisor and told them. My supervisor brought in this person and they proceeded to say that they didn't mean it that way and that they were proud of me. HA! But….this only fed into my own self-doubt and negative thought patterns. Mostly it caused more paralysis, just like the time I was playing the god damned entertainer.

Who the hell was I to quit this job? I could never make it on my own! My education wasn't good enough, I didn't have enough letters behind my name, I was gonna get eaten alive!

It was then that I realized that I needed to practice what I preached and do some real work on my mindset. I needed to destroy my core belief of negative self-worth so I could break free.

Let's talk about fear. The best acronym I have found is False Evidence Appearing Real. Wow, that's a kick to the gut isn't it? I thought all of my fear was and is entirely justified, right? Nope! Most of the time the fear I have doesn't even turn out to be as bad as I made it out to be. Most of my fear has to do with scenarios and worst case outcomes that I make up in my head. Most of the scenarios I make up have to do with negative outcomes of my children (worry about their safety, friendships, finding a seat at the lunch table, eating alone, being alone, etc.) or other people judging me (for anything and all things). All of the energy I have put into the worry and fear does not have an equal outcome to what actually happens. Damn Newton's law! Newton's third law is: For every action, there is an equal and opposite reaction. I suppose I was viewing my fear and worry as the action that would induce the opposite reaction of complete tragedy. Guess what? It NEVER happens the way I think its going to happen with an outcome of pure catastrophe! I have literally had to tell myself, "Everyone is just fine" a lot. Guess what? Everything is just fine!

There was a recent YouTube video circulating about a miniature pony trying to get out of the stable. It was hesitating while jumping up to the edge of the doorway and will prance all around and go back. This happened over and over again until it became courageous enough to jump of the step and into the corral. Once in the corral it bucked and jumped due to what looked like complete elation! See, the anticipation of the actual event caused a tremendous amount of fear even for a little pony.

Another example is the Steve Harvey video where he talks about 'just jumping'. This video hit me like a ton a bricks. He says all of our daily worries will always be there: bills, kids, money. But, if we never take a risk we will never reap a reward. If we never 'jump' from our fear we will never know if our parachute will actually open and catch us. This makes me think of all of the times that my parachute did open. But there were plenty of times that the parachute had somewhat of a delayed response but eventually opened.

Fear is the one thing that has kept me back from living the life that I want. Worry, a close cousin of fear has consumed me, especially with raising my kids.

TESTIMONIAL

I grew up as a latch key kid. You know the ones that came home to an empty house and had to take care of themselves until someone else showed up. I was a latch key kid at the age of six. It was terrifying to come home to an empty house and have to get my own snack and ensure the house was safe until my older brother got there about an hour later. That fear led me to become a stay- at- home- mom as soon as I could. I loved being home, but I also wanted to work. Yet, fear stopped me from working. I never wanted my kids to feel that lonely feeling of no one being there for them. Fear ruled my life for a very long time. It was also fear that led me to follow my heart to become a coach. After years of being a stay- at -home -mom and doing small jobs that allowed me to always be home for my kids, I had that moment of utter fear when I realized my kids were growing up and wouldn't be living at home for much longer. Other than a mom and a wife, I had no idea who I was. What did I like to do? What did I want to spend the rest of my life doing? I realized I no longer wanted to wait to be needed and fear I wouldn't be. Instead, I decided it was time to do for me. Man did that feel selfish!! In the end, I discovered fear is a horrible way to live. That fear lied to me for most of my life. I finally realized I could have it all! The answer to all my questions and fears was trusting myself! Having the confidence to believe I was worth it. That what I wanted mattered.

And even more so, that I could achieve all my dreams. You do too! It's all about believing in yourself more than fear. Believing you have what it takes and gaining the confidence to trust yourself more than your fear.

M.P,

There is a lot of fear around doing something different. Sometimes we are so 'attached' to our anxious stated that we don't really want to let it go. Letting it go might mean not being able to 'get away' with leaving somewhere early or denying and invitations. Letting go of anxiety might just mean that we have to show up to our lives in a new way. That new way creates some fear.

How can we dial down our nervous system and get rid of that fear? How can we change our negative thought patterns and core belief systems?

IT'S VAGUS BABY!

Perhaps you have been hearing about the vagus nerve or maybe you have not. But the vagus nerve runs from the base of your head (think brain stem) all the way down your spine to your bottom. It touches your organs on its way down. It is part of your autonomic nervous system (think things you do automatically without having to think about it like breathing, heart beating and digestion). The brain sends stress hormones up and down this information super highway which is why you might experience butterflies in the gut or a gut instinct. If the vagus nerve is not stimulated you can experience a bunch of problems including but not limited to: anxiety, panic attacks, ringing in the ears, depression, weight gain, bowel and digestive issues and more.

When we are in fight or flight (extreme stress or anxiety) our sympathetic nervous system becomes engaged. However, over time it tends to not dial down adequately to engage the parasympathetic side (think calm and Vagus nerve). So we end up feeling anxious more frequently, unable to relax and begin to look at the world as one big giant threat.

Since we have been 'exercising' our sympathetic nervous system our parasympathetic nervous system has essentially been dormant so to speak. It's kind of like going to the gym and only doing squats. Our thighs would get huge but we would have T-rex arms! The idea is to essentially workout (dial down) our parasympathetic nervous system so we can experience calm again. There are some easy ways to stimulate the vagus nerve. Since the nerve connects everything from the head to your bottom you can stimulate it from both ends.

Here are the top ways to 'workout' the vagus nerve:

- Gargling – Hard gargling (so hard your eyes water) several times a day
- Gagging
- Meditation
- Humming
- Singing
- Breathing
- Massage/reflexology/acupuncture
- Cold water/Cold Showers
- Coffee enemas

Aside from vagus nerve stimulation, there are many ways to dial down our nervous system. But a couple unsung heroes (in my book anyway) are Breathing, EMDR (Eye Movement Desensitization and Reprocessing), Yoga and Mindset. As a therapist myself I use EMDR in my practice all of the time. I really love to partner it with yoga before and after a session. This really helps to center the individual and make sure they are out of their fight/flight response and can carry on. EMDR can be tough no doubt, but it is also extremely effective in uncovering negative core beliefs (I'm worthless, I don't matter, etc.) understanding how the body has held on to those beliefs and destroying them! What do these modalities have in common? They all impact the VAGUS nerve.

BREATHING

I know we breathe every single day. For the most part we don't even think about it, until we do. Our breath is tied to our heart rate. Our heart rate dictates how our nervous system will respond. When our pulse is over 100 beats per minute adrenaline will be released and now we are in fight or flight. When we breathe in our heart rate goes up. When we exhale it will go down. If we have control over our breathing we will have control over our heart rate which means we can gain control over anxiety too! Remember that the exhale is the most important part of your breath so start with a long slow exhale first. Do not take 3 big breaths in and out and think you are done. Your body needs to 'catch on' to the idea that a bear is not chasing you and it's ok to settle down. This take about 5-7 minutes of slow breathing. The type of breathing I like is the meditators breathe.

Start by laying flat on the floor (this will help your breathing). When you take a deep breath with your nose in pretend that you are filling your entire chest cavity with air from the bottom to the top for the count of a slow 4. Now purse your lips together and have a slow, controlled exhale to count of a slow 8. That's it! Continue to do this for 5-7 minutes.

To make things even easier go ahead and download a breathing app. There are tons of them that are absolutely free. Just make sure you can adjust the inhale and exhale counts. Practice breathing multiple times during the day when you aren't anxious. This is important because just like playing a sport you would never show up to game day without practicing a lot. This is no different. Practice this breathing when you don't need it so you can access it when you really do need it.

Your body keeps the score of whatever hurt and pain you have been through. This means that what you have endured physically and emotionally is stored within your body. This causes an entire host of problems to emerge. These issues are often diagnosed as physical pain (fibromyalgia or unresolved pain), emotion pain (such as depression, anxiety and trauma) and a compromised immune system (often sick) and even addictions.

YOGA for MINDSET and STRESS RELIEF

Yoga is a great addition to your life for a number of reasons. Yoga's ability to work with the whole body, mind and spirit makes is very versatile when pursuing a healthier lifestyle. Therapeutic yoga can strengthen and stabilize connective tissue and muscle around bone(s) as well as help with posture and be an outlet for emotional stress, anxiety reduction and improved sleep. There are many different types of yoga instruction. However, eastern yoga is one of the most important ways of instruction as it is yoga as it was intended. If you are searching for a yoga class skip out on exercise, work out type or even hot yoga. If you struggle with anxiety you need to focus on yoga that emphasizes mindfulness, breathing and stretching. This will engage your VAGUS nerve and assist in the calm body and mind response that you are looking for.

 Additionally, remember that yoga is a lifestyle not just a set of poses to contort your body into. Anyone can do yoga regardless of body shape or size and regardless of perceived ability. I look at yoga bit differently than most. When we think of yoga we tend to think of it as spending an hour of time engaging in a class. Oh wait… that class took more than an hour didn't it? You have to get there and get back. Now we are engaging in stress around a yoga class and the loss of time. Instead do yoga and breathing throughout the day. Do you typically have times of day that are more stressful than others? Do yoga then! Use yoga when you need it, not just during a prescribed class.

THOUGHT PATTERNS

Yoga Sutra II.34 states the following: Negative thoughts are violence, etc. They may be personally performed, performed on one's behalf by another, or authorized by oneself; they may be triggered by greed, anger, or delusion; and they may be slight, moderate, or extreme in intensity. One should cultivate counteracting thoughts, namely, that the end results of negative thoughts are ongoing suffering and ignorance.

I think a lot of times anxiety and depression can be environmental. It can be trying to trudge through something in your life that's not working for instance. A house that has become so unkept that you don't know where to start, it's so overwhelming. Or a relationship that's just so toxic. But you refused to get out of it. Or a job that is constant stress. There's the biology or genetic coding of anxiety versus like situational anxiety and then there's a combination of the two things.

I knew that anxiety wasn't a result of poor genetic coding and at one point, I actually had my genetic code tested. A couple of years ago and found out that sure as shit, the anxiety I was experiencing was not written in my genetic code, it was situational.

So really evaluating in your life. What is working, what is not and how can we fix it is important. But, it might not be as important as 'owning' it. What do I mean by that? Well, we use language that is based in ownership of something. When we use phrases like "my anxiety' and "It's my anxiety" basically means that we took ownership of having it. That means I keep it, it is mine. It's always with me instead of saying, "I feel anxious." Or "I'm experiencing anxiety". Do you see the difference?

Additionally using different emotional terminology outside of anxiety such as, "I'm nervous. I have a test coming up. I'm scared. I'm overwhelmed by this task.". I think we have used the term 'anxiety' as a blanked term to describe stress, nervousness, overwhelm and fear. So we really need to begin to piece apart what we really mean by 'anxiety'. Doing that, not accepting ownership by choosing different language options around your anxiety is powerful.

MINDSET

You've probably heard it before, but let's hear it again! Mindset is everything! The fact that brain activity is the most intense when you exhibit a growth mindset shows how important it is that you believe in yourself. A growth mindset is the belief that we never stop learning, never stop growing and we continue to make new neurological pathways. Think of the rose colored glasses scenario. If we put grey glasses on we will look at the world in a negative way. If we put rose glasses on we will experience the world in a positive, kind way. Think about who in your life you put the rose glasses on for and who you don't. Typically we slide those rose glasses on for our kids. Even when they are doing something wrong we love them and forgive them because they are so wonderful! The grey glasses often come on for ourselves. We look in the mirror and see imperfection. We engage in negative belief systems and constantly berate ourselves. Think of this in the middle of an anxiety attack. This is a time when we are at our worst, fearing what will happen berating ourselves for feeling an emotion!

It all starts in your head and the stories you have told yourself over and over again! What do you really want to believe about yourself? Keep it small. It might be "I'm ok" or perhaps "I'm doing my very best". It might be more powerful like "I'm a complete badass". Whatever it is write it on your bathroom mirror, stick a post it note in your car and start saying it! Stop yourself when you say negative things and slip right back into the positive. All of the time spent engaging in negative mindset was self induced. You took a lot of time and energy to do that to perfection! Now…it's time to think something new and create a new positive pathway.

It's kind of like standing in front of a giant wheat field. At the other side of the field is something negative or something positive. You chose to get to the negative side. The first time you cut through the field it was hard. You had to chop down and stomp down the wheat. After a while of traveling that path, you no longer had to chop or stomp because it's a well traveled dirt path and you can just run to negative side really quickly. I'm asking you to stand in front of the wheat field and start the path to the positive side. You know how hard it's going to be. But you aren't afraid of the work. So take that first step and stomp down the wheat! Keep doing this until you are able to freely skip to the positive!

BUT WHAT IF…..

But what if there is nothing positive about me? Trust me girlfriend there is plenty of positive to go around. Make an inventory of positive things you want to believe about yourself. Ask your friends or family to help you out. I know it's scary to leave behind old beliefs. They are like prickly blankets that have kept you warm all of these years. But you don't want a prickly blanket anymore. You want a warm, soft, hug!

MINDSET TESTIMONIAL

My son is my best example of knowing what a positive core belief is. I have so many examples of his positive mindset I could share, but I know this book is only so long. Since middle school he has wanted to play high school football. He was never the typical athlete. He didn't really challenge himself that way because the educational piece of school was always extremely challenging for him. Back in those days he would literally beat himself up (with words) about homework every single day. I had so much anxiety around his education, the worry was very strong. He went to an alternative middle school so his body could calm down a bit and he could refocus. He would continue to ask to play football in high school. The summer in between eighth and ninth grade he started going to the weight room and headed to football practice. Keep in mind this kid had NEVER played a single game of football in his life. He was happy to play what he called 'garbage time' at the end of the 4th quarter his freshman year. Fast forward to his sophomore year, he was improving tremendously. With this improved growth was an improvement with school as well. He was gaining confidence and motivation. During his sophomore year he took a white board marker and wrote on his bathroom mirror "I will be a football starter". He soon added other mantras. I asked him how other kids were doing in the weight room and he replied, "I don't worry about anyone but me, I go in there and out lift everyone". His junior and senior year of high school he was a football starter. Now, he just finished 4 years of playing collegiate football.

Dr. Teralyn

7

I LIKE YOU...AND NAPS

"Me: Let me sleep"
"Brain:lol, no, lets' stay awake and remember every stupid decision you made in your life"
"Me: OK"

Tossing and turning, and tossing and turning. I'm too hot, I'm too cold. I'm so tired, but my brain is making the grocery list and thinking about the stupid meme I saw. Does this sounds remotely familiar? Oh, it gets worse! I'm tired all day and literally day dream about going home, putting on my pajamas and when I finally get to lay in bed for the night...you got it...I can't sleep at all!

I didn't want to forget about a chapter on the importance of sleep. Sleep is a great barometer as to how everything else is going for you. I have yet to hear someone come in with mental health problems and not talk about how shitty their sleep is. Worse yet it that mostly people end up getting a prescription sleep aid, use and over the counter sleep aid or use marijuana or alcohol to help them sleep. None of those actually work. You might 'sleep' but you will not get the restorative sleep your body actually needs. So, now what? Well, let's take a look at some sleep habits first before we add a supplement, or prescription, ok?

Sleep habits are also called, sleep hygiene. It's a weird term, but one that is used to describe the habits we have around sleep. As you are reading this, I'm sure you probably already know some of the 'bad' habits you have developed over time. Or, if you are like me you have had to endure some bad habits of your partner around sleep (mine is the constant TV turned on).

Let's first talk about some culprits of bad sleep. The first culprit is a neurotransmitter imbalance. Your neurotransmitter levels can dictate some of your sleep patterns. Keeping it simple…serotonin creates melatonin. Melatonin help you sleep. So, if your serotonin is imbalanced your melatonin will likely be imbalanced as well. One indicator of serotonin imbalance is having trouble falling asleep. Also, if your dopamine, adrenaline or GABA are imbalanced your sleep will be hijacked too as you probably won't be able to shut your brain off at night to go to sleep. So this would be a great time to reread the chapter on neurotransmitters. I'm not a big believer in supplementing with melatonin. Since serotonin creates melatonin I would rather start with correcting neurotransmitter imbalance and allowing your brain and body to do the work naturally.

If you have trouble staying asleep you might consider a couple of things. First consider magnesium supplementation. Magnesium is a natural relaxer and might help you stay asleep. Secondly if you are suddenly awake and it is 2 AM, it might be a blood sugar imbalance. Try a protein snack before bed or a light protein snack if you wake up. Also you could try some l-glutamine to stabilize blood sugars. This would be a great time to reread the chapter on nutrition focusing on reactive hypoglycemia.

Let's say that you have tried the above mentioned ideas and your sleep is still lacking and you don't feel rested. Now it's time to look at your environment. I put this last as typically there is a reluctance to change routines here. But…if nothing else is helping, this might be what you are needing to do.

Caffeine

You probably know that caffeine is a stimulant. But, you might be caught in the cycle of "I'm so tired in the afternoon that have to drink it to stay awake". I have also heard people say that they are so tired and caffeine doesn't make a difference to their sleep. Well, it does! Not only does caffeine reduce the quality of deep sleep that you get, but it can impact you for more than 24 hours, sometimes for a couple of days. In one study it was found that drinking caffeine 6 hours before bed reduced deep sleep time by 1 hour. Right now you might be saying, so what? But…you are also reading the chapter on sleep, right?? Caffeine has a half life of 3-5 hours. It reaches peak levels in your blood in about 60 minutes. So..let's do the math on that. Lets say you drink 200mg of caffeine at 2pm. You will still have 100mg of caffeine in your system at 8pm and 50mg in your system at 2am and 25mg of caffeine at 8am and so on. So essentially 200mg of caffeine will need almost an entire day to metabolize through your system. But, keep in mind that by 8am you are probably reaching for more. Additionally caffeine impacts your adrenals. If you reach for caffeine upon waking your adrenals (which produce cortisol) become sluggish over time. So, if nothing else, wait on the caffeine (about 2 hours) after you wake up to allow those adrenals to get going first. Or, if sleep is a huge problem for you, eliminate it altogether for a while and see what happens. Caffeine can be found in some sneaky places so make sure that you are reading labels closely.

Alcohol

Many people grab alcohol at the end of a busy day to help them relax and to potentially fall asleep. There was a recent review of literature that totally debunked the idea that alcohol helps you sleep. Yes, alcohol helped people to fall asleep but it impaired the REM and deep sleep cycle. The more you drink, the more pronounced these effects were. Another effect of alcohol is reactive hypoglycemia. Remember the section on blood sugar? Review it quickly. But, essentially alcohol will cause your blood sugar to fall and wake you up when adrenaline starts pumping. So, you might pop out of bed at 2am or just anytime that you consider too early.

Blood Sugar

Making sure that your blood sugar is stabilized before bed is a great way to have a good night's sleep. If you eat sugar or drink alcohol before bed you will experience a spike and dive in blood sugar. Then your adrenaline will kick in and wake you up. How do you combat hypoglycemia? Make sure your blood sugars are stabilized. Instead of reaching for a salty, carby or sugary snack before bed, reach for some protein. If you wake up in the middle of night try a small protein snack bedside or take some l-glutamine. Review the section on reactive hypoglycemia in this book.

Your Room Itself:

Is your room a place of solitude? Or, is your room a catch all for everything? Is it a relaxing place or is it relatively chaotic or even stressful? Start here. Do your clothes have a 'home'? Are your shoes everywhere? Begin to straighten our your environment. Put clothes where they belong, tuck your shoes away and really turn your bedroom into a haven for sleep. There should only be two activities that you do in your bedroom…get sleep and have sex. If you are doing more than those two things, then you need to do some evaluation here.

Your bed/bedding/pillows

It's funny because I talk to people all the time about sleep but rarely do we bring up the bed you actually sleep on. Many people actually choose to sleep on a couch or recliner because their beds are so uncomfortable! But, they don't consider getting a new mattress. Can't afford a new mattress? Get a memory foam mattress topper (not just one of those egg crate toppers either). Once I got a memory foam mattress, my nights changed forever. I used to wake up stiff with a terrible back ache. No more!

Your bedding is another area of consideration. You don't need 15 sheet sets. All you really need is to splurge on one super comfy set of sheets that you can wash and reuse. I will tell you that I would rather splurge on an awesome set of sheets than rotate a few crappy, scratchy sets wouldn't you? In addition to that think about blankets. I love super soft blankets. I also have about 6 blankets on my bed. It's kind of like layers of winter clothes. I can pull up covers or take them off depending upon how hot or cold I am. Finally, don't forget about pillows! If you can't change anything else, change your pillow. There is a difference between a $5 pillow and a $75 pillow. I swore I would never spend that much on a pillow, until I did. Oh Man! That was a game changer! My pillow actually keeps it shape and I keep my comfort all night.

Lights

Shut all of your lights off and take a look around the room. What lights do you see? Maybe the phone charger lights up or the cable box light is lit. What do you see? Blue light suppresses the production of the sleep hormone melatonin more than any other light source. Green lights aren't much better and suppress melatonin about half as much as blue lights. So, it is very important to eliminate as much light as possible in your bedroom.

 Some light sources:

- Blue Lights
- Green Lights
- Phone lights
- Night lights
- Television
- Screens (tablets, reading devices)
- Light coming in from a shadeless window

Telephone ,Tech or TV Use Before Bed

All screens and this in telephones, tablets (tech) and TV interrupts your natural circadian rhythm (sleep wake cycle). They also interfere with serotonin productions. Additionally using technology or TV while in bed causes you to go to bed later and keeps your brain from shutting down (due to stimulation). Cut tech time and TV out 1-2 hours prior to bedtime to improve your sleep quality. I'm telling you now, social media doesn't care as much about your sleep as you care about scrolling through it.

Sounds

Noise can be disrupting to your sleep particularly during certain sleep phases. The phase impacted the most is the falling asleep and beginning sleep phase. Noise can also impact sleep during sleep phase transition such as REM sleep to deep sleep. Noise can prevent you from falling asleep and can wake up after you are asleep. Take a minute to lay in bed with everything off. What do you hear? Perhaps you have a clock ticking or you can hear the dog licking himself. These things might be subtle but worth fixing. Also if the TV or radio is on through the night, you might be disrupting your sleep unknowingly. A final disruption is a partner snoring. Snoring causes a lot of problems for not only the person doing it, but also for the person sharing a room. There are some essential oil blends that can help. So can different pillows, bedding, mattress or even weight loss. But snoring isn't always a weight loss issue. Sometimes it's a medical condition or a sleep hygiene problem. Using a sound conditioner can help with down out noises with white noise. A fan can also do this. But, if you don't need to drown out noises (such as snoring), turn off noise producing items.

Temperature

You are more likely to sleep easier in a cooler environment. Finding the cooler environment is a personal decision. I like to sleep with the house temperature at 62-64 degrees. I layer up my blankets so I can adjust hotter or cooler much easier. My hubby likes a hot sleep environment (but then complains when he wakes up in a sweat) so we do have a heated mattress pad that we can regulate different temperature on each side of the bed.

Routine

Since my kids were little we instilled a good bedtime routine so their little bodies knew when it was time to begin to wind down and fall asleep. The routine was essentially bath, book and bed. If you think about some of the bedtime routines that you have around sleep you can easily pair new routines with the old ones. For instance if you brush your teeth before bed, take a magnesium supplement at the same time or plug your phone in and don't look at it for the night. If you put your phones and technology away (and shut off the TV) this is a great time to reconnect with your partner and with your family too. Finally, don't exercise too close to bedtime. You won't be able to turn your adrenaline down far enough to get you to sleep.

Keep a consistent bedtime and wake up time even on the weekends. I know the bedtime during the week isn't as challenging as on the weekends. But I always think back to my kids when they were little. Their body didn't care if it was Friday night or Wednesday night they were used to the same sleep wake cycle. Your adult body is not different especially during this correction period. So give a consistent sleep wake pattern a try.

My favorite sleep routine (especially on a Sunday night) is to take an Epsom salt bath with vetiver and lavender essential oils. If you can't take a bath try a foot soak. Epsom salts help you detox and relax. I find that Sunday nights are typically the hardest night for me to get to sleep. So this routine is very helpful to me.

Sleep Aids and Supplements

I really never advise to take an over the counter sleep aid or a prescription aid. They are often addictive and you might have trouble sleeping without them. Some natural remedies to try are:

- Essential oils diffused bedside (review the chapter on essential oils)
- Epsom salt baths or foot soaks
- Magnesium supplementation
- A supplement that is designed for natural sleep such as insomnitol
- Consider GABA if you have trouble turning off your brain
- Consider l-Theanine or Taurine as well
- Consult with your care provider for recommended supplementation that fits your needs

What If….

What if you have a partner that doesn't want to change anything about sleep hygiene?

Rest assured (no pun intended) you still have some options. In the spirit of good, better, best…here are some good options.

- Do your best to control your own sleep hygiene first
- Sleep mask (I like yoga eye pillows) if your partner won't turn off the TV or get rid of blue lights
- Ear plugs (if your partner snores or you have noises from the TV or technology in the room)
- Fans – use a fan to create some white noise
- Air conditioning sound machines – use this if your partner doesn't like a fan
- Sleep in a different room that you can create into your sleep haven paradise

8

LET'S GET PHYSICAL

Exercise? I thought you said extra fries!

It wasn't that long ago that I was an exercise fiend. You could constantly find me training for the next race - running 6 half marathons in 2 years time. I was obsessed in the worst ways and didn't give a shit about what my body had to say about it until injury struck. Then I was pissed off. In my all or nothing thinking - I quit. When I say I quit, I mean it. I packed up my shoes, my running gear, everything and just stopped. Now, neither of those options were health in any way. But, I wanted to share with you how the all or nothing thinking gets in the way of everything. I told myself the story of why I couldn't do it anymore and stuck to the story. I couldn't remain flexible. But, in either case I damaged my body and my mind.

At this point, I hate even telling people to exercise. By now you've heard it all but you still feel a little stuck. We know that exercise helps your body, but what can it do for your brain. Do you have to do hard cardio to get there. No. Please don't do that actually because you will do more harm than good. Here are the compelling reasons you need to move more.

Makes You Feel Good: When you exercise, your brain releases endorphins—those "feel-good" chemicals that instantly lift your mood. They're like nature's happy pill, helping to reduce stress, anxiety, and even depression.

Sharpens Your Focus: Exercise gets the blood flowing to your brain, which helps improve the production of dopamine and norepinephrine—neurotransmitters that play a huge role in focus, motivation, and mood regulation. So, not only do you feel better, but you can also think clearer and concentrate better!

Boosts Energy: Even though it may seem like exercise would make you tired, it actually helps your brain produce more serotonin, the neurotransmitter responsible for your sense of well-being and energy. So, by moving your body, you get a natural boost that can keep you energized throughout the day.

Reduces Stress: Exercise also helps lower cortisol levels (the stress hormone), which is great for calming your brain down and helping you relax. This is especially helpful when you're feeling overwhelmed and need a mental reset.

Protects Your Brain: Regular exercise encourages the production of brain-derived neurotrophic factor (BDNF), which supports the growth of new brain cells and helps protect against cognitive decline. So, not only does exercise improve your mood today, but it also helps keep your brain healthy for the future.

Excuses for Not Moving and Why They're Totally Ridiculous (But We Love You Anyway)

"I'm too tired."

Argument: Guess what? Exercise actually gives you more energy! It's like a free battery recharge for your body—plus, you won't be tired *forever*.

"I don't have time."

Argument: I'm pretty sure you spend more time scrolling through memes than you do in your workout. Just sayin'. Try squeezing in a 15-minute walk and see how much more time you have to complain afterward.

"I don't have the right equipment."

Argument: Your body is the only piece of equipment you really need! But if you really want to level up, you can always use a spoon as a dumbbell. (I'm not recommending this, but it's possible.)

"I'm too old for this."

Argument: No such thing as "too old," just "too cool" to move! Also, exercise is scientifically proven to keep you young. Try telling your muscles they're not allowed to age—see what happens.

"I don't like sweating."

Argument: Sweating is just your body's way of saying, "Hey, I'm working hard here!" It's not gross, it's *glowing*. Think of it as a natural highlighter for your face.

"It hurts."

Argument: You know what else hurts? Getting stuck on the couch for hours, feeling like a potato. Plus, exercise makes you tougher. You'll be the one laughing when you can carry all the grocery bags in one trip. (Trust me, that's a power move.)

"I'm not a gym person."

Argument: You don't have to be! Try dancing in your kitchen or doing yoga in your living room. No one's judging you, and your cat's probably impressed.

"I'll look silly."

Argument: So what? Everyone looks a little goofy when they're trying something new. Besides, your body won't care if you're doing the "awkward chicken dance"—it'll just appreciate the movement.

"I can't do it perfectly."

Argument: Perfect is overrated. Think of it like learning to cook—you're not Gordon Ramsay the first time, but you still get to eat! Just move, however you can, and the rest will follow.

"I don't feel like it."

Argument: Fair enough. But you know what feels even worse? Waking up one day and realizing you can't touch your toes anymore. Get up, move, and avoid future regret.

Walking: The Easiest Exercise You've Been Avoiding (But You Shouldn't)"

So, you've been thinking about getting active, but the thought of hitting the gym makes you want to nap instead? Well, good news—walking is here to save the day! It's like exercise for people who don't want to sweat, lift weights, or learn complicated moves. All you have to do is put one foot in front of the other—and keep doing that for a while. It's that simple, and guess what? It's packed with benefits for your body and brain. So, lace up those sneakers, and let's talk about why walking might just be the easiest (and most rewarding) thing you can do today!

Walking is like the superhero of exercises—easy, low-impact, and packed with benefits! Here's why taking a stroll is actually one of the best things you can do for your body and brain:

1. **Boosts Your Mood**: Walking gets your blood pumping, which means more oxygen for your brain. This leads to the release of feel-good chemicals like endorphins and serotonin. Translation: you feel happier and less stressed!

2. **Improves Heart Health**: It's good for your ticker! Walking strengthens your heart, lowers your blood pressure, and helps reduce the risk of heart disease. Plus, it's a great way to keep your circulation flowing smoothly.

3. **Supports Weight Management**: Walking may not feel like a calorie-torching workout, but it adds up! Regular walks can help maintain a healthy weight, and combined with healthy eating, it's a simple way to stay on track.

4. **Boosts Energy Levels**: A quick walk can actually increase your energy levels by improving circulation and oxygen flow throughout your body. Forget the coffee—try a walk next time you hit that afternoon slump!

5. **Improves Digestion**: A good walk after meals helps your digestive system work more efficiently. It can reduce bloating, help with digestion, and make you feel more comfortable post-meal.

6. **Sharpens Your Mind**: Walking boosts brain function by increasing blood flow to the brain, improving memory, focus, and mental clarity. It's like a mental reset for your brain.

7. **Strengthens Muscles and Bones**: Walking works your leg muscles, improves your posture, and strengthens bones. It can even help prevent bone loss as you age, especially when done regularly.

8. **Promotes Better Sleep**: Regular walking can help you sleep better. It calms your body, reduces stress, and regulates your circadian rhythm, making it easier to fall asleep and stay asleep.

9. **Improves Balance and Coordination**: Regular walking improves your overall balance, making you less prone to falls. It's like a free balance-training session every time you step outside.

10. **It's Free and Easy**: You don't need a gym membership, fancy equipment, or even a lot of time. Just put on your shoes and go for a walk around the block. No excuses!

If you've ever tried to start a new habit, you know it can be tricky. But what if I told you there's a way to make walking a regular part of your day without much effort? Enter **habit stacking**—the secret weapon to building routines without the overwhelm. The idea is simple: stack your new habit (walking) on top of something you already do every day. For example, every time you finish your morning coffee, you immediately go for a 5-minute walk. Easy, right?

Now, let's throw in a **step counter** (or fitness tracker, if you're fancy). This is your new best friend. Start by checking how many steps you're currently getting in a day. Don't stress if the number is low—this is your baseline. Once you know where you're starting, the goal is to gradually increase your steps by adding a few more each day or week. Use your step counter as a motivator—each time you check it, you'll see how much closer you're getting to your goal!

Here's the cool part: By pairing your new walking habit with something you already do, you're not just creating a new routine— you're literally building new **neural pathways** in your brain. When you take action and start preparing for the walk, your brain begins to form connections that make this activity feel more natural over time. Essentially, the more you prepare for and take action on the walk, the more your brain recognizes it as part of your regular routine. Before you know it, walking will become second nature.

You can stack this habit anywhere in your routine—before lunch, after dinner, or as a break between meetings. Each time you check in with your step counter, you'll feel that little boost of achievement. And over time, as you keep adding those steps, you'll build the walking habit without even thinking about it. Who knew health could be so easy (and so data-driven)?

In short, walking is one of the simplest, most accessible ways to improve your health and well-being. It's good for your body, good for your brain, and good for your mood—all without breaking a sweat. So, why not take a walk? It's literally a step in the right direction!

9

LIFE IS SO DAMN SHORT, JUST DO WHAT MAKES YOU HAPPY

"Don't forget to shout "JENGA" when everything falls apart"
JFisherjewelry

I stumbled upon happiness as a field of study because I was miserable. Let me back that story up a bit for you. I was working in the prison, was living an unhealthy life and it showed. I was approached by a social worker who declared that I was one of the most negative people they had ever met. Of course, my defense when off like a 5 alarm fire. After stewing in this information for a while. I got curious and courageous. I started to ask other people what they thought of me. Guess what…I repeatedly got the same answer. I was negative and didn't know it. Or maybe I did know it but felt justified in it somehow. Apparently I dismissed ideas, poked holes in other ideas and acted like a know it all. I thought I was advocating for people but instead I was creating road blocks. So, I dove headfirst into the study of happiness.

I even conducted original research and wrote my entire PhD dissertation on the topic. Did I get happier? I think I did, but I constantly check myself.

HAPPINESS

Happiness is more like a state of being than a fleeing moment of joy. Happiness, is a bit of a struggle sometimes isn't it? Everyone searches for it, but people have such trouble finding it. There are a ton of books written about happiness but my favorites are anything by Martin Seligman. He is the master of happiness and positive psychology. His approach is relatively simple, and I'm paraphrasing here:

1. Express gratitude – tell others what you are grateful for and keep a gratitude journal
2. Find little bits of happiness frequently – every single day notice the smallest things that bring you joy.
3. Savor moments – smell the coffee, take your time

Express Gratitude – Tell People What You're Thankful For (And Keep a Journal, Too)

Gratitude is like your brain's cheat code for feeling better, but here's the catch—it's gotta be real. Sure, you can be thankful for the big things like a promotion or a fresh paycheck, but the true magic happens when you start appreciating the little things. That random text from a friend, your morning coffee that doesn't taste like dirt, or the way your dog looks at you like you're their entire world. These moments? Gold.

Telling people what you're thankful for—whether it's your partner who made you a sandwich or your coworker who didn't steal your lunch—helps you connect and build those feel-good vibes. Seriously, try it. You'll feel lighter, and they'll think you're a hero. Then, there's the gratitude journal. No, it's not as lame as it sounds. Start jotting down three things you're grateful for every day, even if it's just the fact that you got through your email inbox without crying. Over time, your brain gets rewired to focus on the positive stuff. Try it for a week, and you'll see your mood (and possibly your social life) improve.

Find Little Bits of Happiness Every Damn Day – It's in the Details, Dude

We're so busy looking for the big "ah-ha" moments of joy that we miss all the little sparks of happiness happening around us. It's the tiny stuff—like hearing your favorite song on the radio, that perfect nap in the sun, or finding that last piece of chocolate in the cupboard. All those little moments? They count. But you have to be awake enough to notice them. Seriously, don't just speed through your day like you're on autopilot. Take a second to be like, "Hey, that was awesome."

We're talking about the stuff that lights you up without needing a massive life change. Did you catch that stunning sunset? That's happiness. Found a cool rock on your walk? That's joy. The more you start noticing these things, the more your brain gets hooked on the good stuff. It's like planting tiny seeds of happiness that grow into a garden of better vibes. So, go ahead—celebrate the little wins. They're basically the secret sauce to feeling good every day.

Savor the Moments – Slow the Hell Down and Actually Enjoy Your Life

Look, we all live in fast forward mode, rushing from one thing to the next, as if we're in some race we didn't sign up for. But guess what? Life's not a checklist, and you're not getting paid by the minute. So, what if you just slowed down and *actually* enjoyed something for once? Savoring isn't just a fancy word for foodies—it's about truly experiencing the moment, and it's surprisingly powerful.

Smell that coffee—really *smell* it. Take a slow bite of your lunch, and notice how the flavors hit your taste buds. Heck, take five minutes to just listen to the sounds around you, or feel the wind on your face. When you savor moments like this, you're fully present, and it's like your brain gets a reset. No more "what's next?" anxiety. Just "this is enough." It's not about rushing through life; it's about actually living it. So next time, ditch the phone and just *be* in the moment. Trust me, it makes life way more fun.

How Changing Your Perspective Changes Your Mental Health and Brain

Changing your perspective isn't just a feel-good concept—it can actually reshape how your brain functions and has a powerful impact on your mental health. When you look at the world differently, you start wiring your brain to respond differently. It's not just about thinking positively; it's about giving your brain the freedom to approach challenges with a fresh outlook, which can literally change your mental state.

Here's how it works: Your brain has a concept called neuroplasticity, which is its ability to rewire itself in response to new experiences, thoughts, and behaviors. When you change how you view situations—whether they're problems, challenges, or opportunities—your brain begins to form new connections. If you start to see a setback as a chance to learn rather than a failure, your brain will gradually shift to focus on growth and solutions. Over time, your brain gets better at handling adversity with less stress and anxiety.

The way you think about stress and anxiety also plays a massive role in mental health. If you constantly see stress as something overwhelming, your body and brain are going to react accordingly, increasing cortisol levels (your stress hormone) and keeping you stuck in that "fight or flight" mode. But if you change your perspective on stress, viewing it as something manageable or even motivating, your brain can trigger more positive reactions, like increased focus and energy. This shift helps lower cortisol and boost mental clarity and resilience.

Plus, when you reframe negative thoughts, you help activate parts of your brain associated with positivity and emotional regulation. Your prefrontal cortex, which handles decision-making, problem-solving, and emotional control, starts to work more efficiently. Meanwhile, the amygdala—the part of your brain responsible for fear and negative emotions—becomes less reactive. This creates a calmer mental state, helping you handle stress and anxiety better.

Changing perspective also influences your mood. When you start seeing things in a more optimistic light, you're encouraging the production of neurotransmitters like serotonin and dopamine, which are the brain's "feel-good" chemicals. This can improve your overall mood and sense of well-being. Plus, it helps with motivation—when you see things from a more hopeful standpoint, you're more likely to take action and make positive changes.

At the end of the day, altering your perspective isn't just a mental exercise; it's a brain exercise. It strengthens neural pathways that promote calmness, positivity, and growth, all of which are essential for better mental health. So, the next time you're facing a tough situation, remember: Changing how you view it isn't just about thinking differently—it's literally reshaping your brain for the better.

Change Your Perspective, Change Your Life

Here's the truth: your perspective is everything. How you see the world, your circumstances, and even yourself shapes the life you lead. If you're stuck in a loop of negativity, everything will seem like a roadblock. But shift your perspective, and suddenly, the world is full of possibilities. Sounds simple, right? It really is.

Let's break it down: when you look at challenges, are they problems or opportunities for growth? When you face a setback, do you see it as failure, or do you see it as a lesson in the making? It's all about how you frame it. If you're constantly thinking, "I can't do this," you're putting yourself in a box. But if you think, "How can I make this work?" you're opening the door to creative solutions, new pathways, and, most importantly, progress.

Changing your perspective isn't about forcing yourself to see everything through rose-colored glasses. It's not about ignoring tough situations or pretending everything is sunshine and rainbows. It's about reframing your challenges so you can handle them with a clearer mind. Life happens. You can't control everything, but you can control how you respond. And that response? It's what determines the quality of your life.

For example, think about the last time you faced a tough situation. What would have happened if, instead of thinking "this is impossible," you asked yourself, "How can I turn this into an opportunity?" What if you saw that setback as a stepping stone rather than a stumbling block? That slight shift in how you think can spark a ripple effect of positive changes in every area of your life.

Changing your perspective also means giving yourself the grace to see your own potential. How many times have you sold yourself short, thinking you weren't good enough or capable enough to achieve something? Changing your perspective can break down those limiting beliefs and replace them with confidence and drive.

So, how do you do it? Start small. When life throws a curveball, ask yourself, "What's the lesson here?" or "What can I learn from this?" Over time, you'll notice that your mindset begins to shift naturally. Instead of feeling defeated by obstacles, you'll start to look for the silver linings and opportunities they bring.

Here's the bottom line: Life isn't always going to go the way you want, but how you see it will make all the difference. Change your perspective, and you'll change your life—one thought at a time. It's that simple.

Find Your Strength, Align It with Your Values, and Watch Your Life Get Real

Alright, let's get real for a minute. If you want your life to actually *mean* something, it's time to figure out what you're really good at and what matters to you. Spoiler alert: if you don't know these two things, you're basically just wandering around aimlessly hoping for some kind of cosmic sign to tell you what to do. Newsflash: the sign isn't coming. It's on you.

So, how do you stop fumbling in the dark and start living with purpose? Simple—figure out your personal strengths and line them up with your values. When you do that, you unlock a level of energy and fulfillment that makes everything else feel like it's *actually* worth doing.

Discover Your Strengths

Let's start with you. Yeah, you. Think about what you're really good at. Not the stuff you *think* you should be good at, but the things that come naturally. Maybe you're that person who can solve any problem in a snap, or maybe you've got the charm to connect with anyone you meet. Whatever it is, own it.

Look at your past wins—what made you proud? What do people come to you for advice on? If you're the go-to friend for relationship advice, that's your strength. If you're always the one calming people down in a crisis, that's your strength. Start paying attention to the stuff that gives you energy, not drains you. And if you're still not sure, ask people around you what they think you're best at. Trust me, they'll have answers. Take the VIA signature strength quiz, it might be helpful here.

Know Your Core Values

Now, let's talk values. These are the things that matter to you so much, they could be tattooed on your soul (figuratively, of course). Values are your guiding principles—the stuff you will always stand up for. Maybe it's honesty, maybe it's freedom, maybe it's helping others. But you need to get clear on what they are because when you live in line with your values, life just clicks.

Think about the times when you've felt *really* alive. What were you doing? Who were you with? Chances are, that's when you were living in line with your values. Write down the things that light you up—those are your non-negotiables.

Align Your Strengths with Your Values

Here's where the magic happens. Take what you're *really good at* and start using it to express what you *care about*. When you do that, it's like you've hit the jackpot.

Alright, let's break this down. You're struggling with sleep—totally exhausted but finding yourself glued to your phone at night. You value quality time with your family and absolutely love being present with them, but the lack of sleep is keeping you from showing up the way you want to. And you've got that one strength: consistency. You're a creature of habit, and you do well with routines—especially when it comes to sleep hygiene. But here's the twist: the doom scrolling habit at night is like the ultimate sabotage.

It's the "me time" you've convinced yourself you need, but it's literally draining the life out of you. You're trading hours of potential rest for a cycle of anxiety, sluggishness, and poor sleep that drags into the next day. And when you think about it? It's out of alignment with your values—especially the value of time. Doom scrolling might feel like a way to decompress, but it's actually wasting the precious time you value so much, and making the very thing you want (energy to engage with your family) harder to achieve.

So, let's get creative here.

Recognize the Disconnect

First things first, let's acknowledge that doom scrolling is more of a quick fix than a long-term solution. It's feeding your anxiety but not actually addressing it. And it's making it harder for you to show up as the person you want to be with your family. Recognizing this is the first step in creating change.

Combine Your Strengths with Your Values

You've got the consistency thing down, so let's use that. Instead of scrolling for hours, let's put that consistency to use in a way that truly honors your time. You can create a new, more supportive nighttime routine that still gives you a chance to unwind without sabotaging your sleep or stealing from the time you truly value.

The New Plan

1. **Set a clear intention**: Before you even reach for your phone, set an intention for how you want to end your day. This can be something like: *"I want to wind down in a way that feels peaceful and prepares me for a restful sleep so I can fully enjoy time with my family tomorrow."*

2. **Create a new wind-down ritual**: Ditch the phone and create a routine that actually supports your sleep. Try reading a book (not on your phone!), doing some light stretching, or practicing relaxation techniques. Maybe even a 5-minute gratitude journal to remind yourself of all the good things that happened during the day. This will soothe your mind, and over time, help rewire your brain to associate that end-of-day routine with relaxation, not anxiety.

3. **Time-block for yourself**: Instead of aimlessly scrolling, give yourself some guilt-free "me time" earlier in the day. Maybe after dinner, you take a walk, or carve out a moment for a hobby you enjoy—this way, you're still getting that personal space you crave, just at a time that doesn't mess with your sleep.

4. **Set a tech curfew**: This is a game-changer. Set a tech curfew for yourself—say, 30 minutes before you plan to sleep, no screens. You can use this time to prepare for bed in a way that's calming, like practicing deep breathing, journaling, or even having a relaxing conversation with your partner. This helps reduce anxiety and signals to your brain that it's time to relax, not to amp up.

Aligning Sleep with Your Values

By making these shifts, you're honoring your value of time. You're making sure that the time you do have for yourself is spent in a way that doesn't sabotage your energy for the next day. And by addressing the real need (anxiety), you're able to turn your evenings into a true moment of rest instead of wasting time scrolling, which only leaves you more drained.

The beauty of this approach is that it taps into what you're good at—consistency—and pairs it with what truly matters to you—time with your family. As you create a routine that supports both your mental health and your physical well-being, you're starting to show up as the person you want to be—alert, energized, and ready to fully engage with the ones you love.

So, let's do this. Step away from the scroll and embrace a plan that gives you *real* "me time" that serves you, your family, and the things you value most.

The point is, your strengths aren't just cool talents—they're clues about where you should be focusing your energy. When you use those strengths in ways that align with what matters to you, that's when you start living your best life.

Keep It Real and Live in Alignment

Here's the thing: this isn't some one-and-done checklist. It's a lifestyle. Life changes. You change. So does your sense of what's important. But if you're paying attention and staying true to what you're good at and what lights your fire, things start to fall into place.

Living in alignment with your strengths and values means making decisions that come from your *true self*, not some half-baked version of who you think you're supposed to be. It's about making sure that the stuff you're pouring your time and energy into actually feels *worth it*.

When you're in alignment, life doesn't feel like a grind. You stop going through the motions and start making moves that matter. It's about *thriving*, not just surviving. So get to work on figuring out your strengths, get clear on your values, and start living like you mean it.

Here's the deal: you want a life that actually feels good? Don't just wait for it to happen. Make it happen by aligning your strengths with your values. When you do, you'll not only feel more fulfilled—you'll feel unstoppable.

Alright, so here's the kicker: happiness doesn't just show up because you cross some magic finish line. It's not about waiting for the perfect job, the perfect relationship, or the perfect moment. Happiness comes when you align who you are with what you do and how you see the world. It's all about perspective.

When you figure out your strengths and line them up with your values, you shift your perspective. Instead of feeling stuck or like you're just going through the motions, you start seeing every day as an opportunity to live in alignment with who you really are. And that's when things start to click. The happier you are with what you're doing, the more positive energy you attract into your life. You begin to see things through a lens of gratitude, possibility, and fulfillment.

Now, don't get me wrong—life's still going to throw curveballs, and not every day is going to feel like sunshine and rainbows. But when you're aligned with your true self, your *perspective* shifts. You start to see setbacks as learning opportunities, challenges as growth, and even tough days as stepping stones to the life you want to create.

And here's the thing—when you're truly aligned, happiness isn't just a fleeting moment; it becomes part of your story. You stop chasing after it like some distant dream and start experiencing it every single day, no matter where you are or what you're doing. That's when you can finally look at your life and say, "Yeah, this is the story I wanted to tell."

Happiness, perspective, and alignment? They're the real game-changers. They don't just transform your day—they transform your entire life story. So, if you're ready for a new chapter, start with this: find your strengths, know your values, and align the two. Then, watch your life shift in ways you never thought possible.

10

HELL YEAH!

"You did not come this far to walk away without the victory"
hplyrikz.com

First of all, congratulations! By picking up this book and dedicating yourself to making positive changes, you've already accomplished something incredible. You've taken the time to understand how your brain, body, and habits are all interconnected, and you're now equipped with the tools to create lasting change in your life. You've learned how to tackle challenges head-on, how to realign your habits with your values, and how to nourish your body and brain for optimal health. This journey wasn't just about reading a book—it's about investing in yourself and your future.

Throughout this book, we've explored how your thoughts, behaviors, and choices shape your physical and mental well-being. From understanding the powerful role of nutrition, exercise, and sleep to mastering the art of changing your perspective, we've covered a lot of ground. You've discovered how to support your neurotransmitters, manage stress, build better habits, and, most importantly, shift your mindset in a way that opens the door to greater happiness, energy, and fulfillment. You're now on a path that will lead to a life that is more aligned with your true values and desires.

The Power of Perspective and Action

What we've learned is simple: *change your perspective, change your life.* Your mindset is everything. When you view challenges as opportunities to grow and align your actions with your core values, everything shifts. The tools and strategies in this book are designed to help you do just that—take control of your journey, one conscious decision at a time. But, it's not just about theory; it's about taking action. You've learned that nothing happens without the commitment to follow through.

As you continue to apply these insights in your life, remember that progress is a process. You're going to have moments of success, and you're going to have moments that feel like setbacks—but that's all part of the journey. The key is to keep moving forward, adjust as needed, and be kind to yourself along the way.

Your Next Steps

Now that you've made it through, it's time to take everything you've learned and put it into practice. Begin by focusing on the areas that matter most to you—whether that's improving your mental health, boosting your energy levels, or strengthening your relationships. Take small, consistent steps, and don't be afraid to revisit the strategies in this book whenever you need a little extra guidance. Remember, this is your journey, and you get to decide the pace.

You've got the power to make meaningful changes. Your brain and body are capable of so much more than you might realize, and with a little intention and the right support, there's no limit to what you can achieve. Keep believing in yourself, trust the process, and enjoy the ride.

Stay Connected

I would love to hear how you're doing! If you've had success using any of the techniques in this book, or if you have feedback to share, please reach out. Whether it's sharing your progress or giving suggestions on how to make this book even better, I'm all ears. You can connect with me through my website or social media, where I'll continue to share updates, tips, and new content to keep you motivated and inspired.

You're not in this alone, and I can't wait to see how you continue to grow and thrive. Congratulations again on taking this big step, and remember—your journey has only just begun!

APPENDIX

8-WEEK LIFE CLEAN-UP PLAN

This 8-week plan is designed to help you clean up your life by focusing on eating better, moving more, sleeping better, and thinking differently. Each week will introduce simple, actionable steps that build on each other to help you create lasting changes. The goal is to improve your overall well-being, energy levels, mindset, and health.

Week 1:

Eating Better – Start with Hydration and Whole Foods

Focus: Hydration & Whole Foods

Goal: Improve hydration, eat more whole foods, and reduce processed foods.

- **Action Steps:**

  - Drink at least 8 cups (64 oz) of water daily. If you're struggling, start with a glass first thing in the morning and keep a water bottle with you throughout the day.

  - Replace one processed snack or meal with a whole food alternative (e.g., veggies and hummus, fruit with nuts).

  - Eliminate sugary drinks (soda, flavored coffee, etc.). Replace with water, herbal teas, or sparkling water.

- **Mindset Tip:** Remind yourself that every small change adds up. It's not about perfection—it's about progress.

Week 2:

Move More – Walk Every Day

~ 140 ~

Focus: Movement

Goal: Build the habit of daily physical activity.

- **Action Steps:**

  - Aim for at least 20 minutes of walking every day. You can split it up into two 10-minute walks if needed.

  - Track your steps with a fitness tracker or step counter to hold yourself accountable.

  - Use habit stacking: Walk after meals or in between work tasks to fit movement into your routine.

- **Mindset Tip:** Exercise doesn't have to mean a tough workout. Start simple, and remember, moving is better than not moving at all!

Week 3:

Sleep Better – Create a Sleep Routine

Focus: Sleep Hygiene

Goal: Improve the quality of your sleep.

- **Action Steps:**

  - Set a consistent bedtime and wake-up time, even on weekends.

  - Avoid screens (phones, TV, computers) at least 30 minutes before bed to help your body wind down.

  - Create a calming bedtime ritual (e.g., reading, deep breathing, or stretching).

- **Mindset Tip:** Sleep is as important for your body and mind as nutrition and exercise. Think of it as a crucial step in self-care.

Week 4:

Think Differently – Practice Gratitude

Focus: Mindset

Goal: Start developing a positive mindset by focusing on gratitude.

- **Action Steps:**
    - Every day, write down 3 things you're grateful for. They can be big or small—anything that makes you feel good.
    - Share your gratitude with others. Send a text or make a quick call to express appreciation for someone.

- **Mindset Tip:** Focusing on what you have (instead of what you don't) can shift your perspective and boost your mood.

Week 5:

Eating Better – Reduce Sugar & Processed Foods

Focus: Nutrition

Goal: Cut down on sugar and processed food intake.

- **Action Steps:**

    - Cut out one processed snack or meal each day. Opt for healthier, nutrient-dense alternatives.

    - Replace sugary desserts with fruit or try dark chocolate if you need a sweet treat.

    - Read labels: Aim to reduce foods with added sugars and focus on whole ingredients.

- **Mindset Tip:** You're not depriving yourself—you're nourishing your body with better options that will fuel you in the long run.

Week 6:

Move More – Add Strength Training

Focus: Exercise

Goal: Introduce strength training into your routine.

- **Action Steps:**

    o   Add two days of strength training (using bodyweight exercises like squats, push-ups, lunges) to your week.

    o   Start with 10-15 minute sessions, focusing on form and gradually increasing repetitions as you get stronger.

    o   Consider a beginner workout video or an app to guide you through exercises.

- **Mindset Tip:** Strength training isn't just about building muscles—it's about feeling empowered and increasing your physical confidence.

Week 7:

Sleep Better – Optimize Your Sleep Environment

Focus: Sleep

Goal: Make your sleep environment more conducive to rest.

- **Action Steps:**
  - Make your bedroom a sanctuary for sleep: dim the lights, keep it cool, and remove distractions like electronics.
  - Try a sleep aid like lavender essential oils or a sleep mask if you find it hard to relax.
  - Reduce caffeine intake after 2 PM and avoid alcohol before bed, as it can disrupt your sleep cycle.
- **Mindset Tip:** A peaceful environment helps tell your body it's time to relax. Make your bedroom a place where sleep feels inviting.

Week 8:

Think Differently – Practice Mindfulness and Positive Self-Talk

Focus: Mindfulness & Self-Talk

Goal: Strengthen your mental resilience by practicing mindfulness and improving self-talk.

- **Action Steps:**

  - Practice a 5-minute mindfulness exercise each morning (e.g., deep breathing, meditation, or mindful walking).

  - Replace negative self-talk with positive affirmations. If you catch yourself thinking "I can't do this," flip it to "I am capable and strong."

  - Start a journaling habit to explore your thoughts and feelings.

- **Mindset Tip:** The way you talk to yourself matters. Shift the narrative to one that supports growth, kindness, and resilience.

Final Thoughts:

Congratulations on completing the 8-week Life Clean-Up! You've laid the foundation for a healthier, more balanced life. As you move forward, remember to keep up with these habits and continue to build on the progress you've made. This isn't a one-time fix; it's a way of living that will continue to support your health, happiness, and well-being for years to come.

GOOD MOOD BRAIN FOOD

Here's a comprehensive list of brain-boosting foods, categorized to help you support optimal brain function. These foods are rich in nutrients that help with memory, focus, mood regulation, and overall cognitive health.

1. Omega-3 Rich Foods (for Brain Structure & Memory)

- Salmon
- Sardines
- Mackerel
- Chia Seeds
- Flaxseeds
- Walnuts
- Hemp Seeds
- Algal Oil (plant-based omega-3s)
- Anchovies

2. Antioxidant-Rich Foods (for Protecting the Brain from Damage)

- **Blueberries** (contain anthocyanins, antioxidants)

- **Dark Chocolate** (70% cocoa or more)

- **Green Tea** (rich in EGCG antioxidants)

- **Spinach** (rich in vitamins C and E)

- **Kale**

- **Broccoli**

- **Beets** (increase blood flow to the brain)

- **Turmeric** (contains curcumin, a powerful anti-inflammatory compound)

- **Cranberries**

- **Pomegranates**

- **Goji Berries**

3. Foods Rich in B Vitamins (for Cognitive Function & Mood Regulation)

- **Eggs** (especially the yolks, high in B vitamins like B12 and folate)

- **Leafy Greens** (spinach, kale, Swiss chard—high in folate)

- **Liver** (beef or chicken)

- **Fortified Cereals**

- **Oats**

- **Sunflower Seeds**

- **Nutritional Yeast** (great for B12)

- **Chickpeas** (rich in folate)

- **Salmon** (B6, B12)

- **Pistachios**

- **Avocados** (B6 and folate)

4. Vitamin D-Rich Foods (for Brain Mood Regulation)

- **Fatty Fish** (salmon, mackerel, sardines, tuna)

- **Egg Yolks**

- **Mushrooms** (especially those exposed to sunlight like maitake, shiitake, and portobello)

- **Fortified Foods** (milk, orange juice, plant-based milk)

- **Cod Liver Oil**

- **Cheese** (but limit processed cheese)

- **Beef Liver**

5. Magnesium-Rich Foods (for Relaxation and Memory)

- **Dark Chocolate** (high-quality, 70% or more)
- **Spinach**
- **Pumpkin Seeds**
- **Almonds**
- **Avocados**
- **Black Beans**
- **Tofu**
- **Bananas**
- **Cashews**
- **Chard**

6. Protein-Rich Foods (for Neurotransmitter Production)

- **Chicken Breast**
- **Turkey**
- **Grass-fed Beef**
- **Tofu**
- **Lentils**
- **Chickpeas**
- **Eggs**
- **Greek Yogurt**
- **Cottage Cheese**
- **Quinoa**
- **Edamame**
- **Nuts and Seeds** (especially walnuts, almonds, and flaxseeds)

7. Foods High in Choline (for Memory and Cognitive Function)

- **Eggs** (especially the yolk)

- **Liver**

- **Salmon**

- **Chicken**

- **Soybeans**

- **Brussels Sprouts**

- **Broccoli**

- **Cabbage**

8. Foods with Healthy Fats (for Brain Function & Protecting Neurons)

- **Olive Oil**

- **Avocados**

- **Nuts** (walnuts, almonds, cashews)

- **Chia Seeds**

- **Flaxseeds**

- **Coconut Oil** (in moderation)

- **Fatty Fish** (salmon, sardines, mackerel)

- **Nut Butters** (peanut butter, almond butter, etc.)

- **Eggs**

- **Hemp Seeds**

9. Foods for Gut Health (Gut-Brain Connection)

- **Fermented Foods** (yogurt, kimchi, sauerkraut, kefir, miso)

- **Prebiotic Foods** (garlic, onions, leeks, asparagus, bananas, apples, oats)

- **Bone Broth** (rich in collagen and amino acids)

- **Chia Seeds**

- **Flaxseeds**

- **Apples** (contain prebiotics)

- **Kimchi**

- **Kefir**

- **Kombucha**

10. Hydration for Cognitive Performance

- **Water** (stay hydrated throughout the day!)

- **Coconut Water** (electrolyte-rich)

- **Herbal Teas** (especially peppermint, ginger, and chamomile)

- **Green Tea** (contains caffeine and L-theanine for focus)

- **Vegetable Juices** (especially fresh green juices)

- **Cucumber** (high water content)

- **Watermelon**

11. Brain-Boosting Spices

- **Turmeric** (contains curcumin, which is anti-inflammatory)

- **Cinnamon** (supports healthy blood sugar)

- **Ginger** (supports circulation to the brain)

- **Rosemary** (studies suggest it may improve memory and focus)

- **Black Pepper** (helps with the absorption of curcumin in turmeric)

- **Saffron** (shown to help with mood regulation and brain function)

- **Ginseng** (supports mental energy and cognitive performance)

By incorporating these brain-boosting foods into your diet, you're giving your brain the fuel it needs to function at its best. From supporting memory and mood to enhancing focus and protecting your brain from damage, these foods will help you keep your mind sharp, your energy levels up, and your overall well-being thriving. Eating for brain health isn't just a trend; it's a lifestyle choice that pays off in the long run!

BRAIN FOOD RECIPES

Here are **10 high-protein brain food recipes** that support neurotransmitter health, each with 4 or fewer ingredients and packed with nutrients essential for your brain. These recipes also highlight key cofactors to support neurotransmitters like serotonin, dopamine, and GABA!

1. Avocado & Tuna Salad

Ingredients:

- 1 ripe avocado
- 1 can of wild-caught tuna
- 1 tablespoon olive oil
- A pinch of sea salt

Instructions:

1. Mash the avocado and mix it with the drained tuna.
2. Drizzle olive oil and season with sea salt.
3. Stir together and serve!

Why it's good for you: Tuna is a great source of protein and omega-3s (important for dopamine production). Avocados provide healthy fats, supporting serotonin and GABA pathways.

Key Nutrients:

- **Dopamine**: Omega-3s from tuna
- **Serotonin**: Healthy fats from avocado
- **GABA**: Magnesium from tuna and avocado

2. Greek Yogurt & Almond Butter Bowl

Ingredients:

- 1 cup Greek yogurt
- 1 tablespoon almond butter
- 1 tablespoon chia seeds

Instructions:

1. Spoon the Greek yogurt into a bowl.
2. Top with almond butter and chia seeds.
3. Stir to combine and enjoy!

Why it's good for you: Greek yogurt is high in protein, providing amino acids like tryptophan, a precursor to serotonin. Almond butter adds healthy fats, which are key for neurotransmitter synthesis.

Key Nutrients:

- **Serotonin**: Tryptophan from Greek yogurt
- **Dopamine**: Healthy fats from almond butter
- **GABA**: Magnesium from chia seeds

3. Chicken & Spinach Salad

Ingredients:

- 1 grilled chicken breast

- 1 cup spinach

- 1 tablespoon olive oil

- Lemon juice for flavor

Instructions:

1. Grill the chicken breast and slice it.

2. Toss spinach in olive oil and lemon juice.

3. Top with sliced chicken and enjoy.

Why it's good for you: Chicken is a high-quality source of protein, providing essential amino acids like tyrosine for dopamine production. Spinach is rich in folate, supporting neurotransmitter function.

Key Nutrients:

- **Dopamine**: Tyrosine from chicken

- **Serotonin**: Folate from spinach

- **GABA**: Vitamin B6 from spinach

4. Hard-Boiled Eggs & Kale

Ingredients:

- 2 hard-boiled eggs

- 1/2 cup sautéed kale

- 1 tablespoon olive oil

Instructions:

1. Hard-boil the eggs and slice them.

2. Sauté kale in olive oil until wilted.

3. Combine the eggs and kale on a plate.

Why it's good for you: Eggs are rich in choline, which is crucial for memory and acetylcholine production. Kale is full of magnesium, which is essential for GABA function.

Key Nutrients:

- **Serotonin**: Choline from eggs

- **Dopamine**: B-vitamins from kale

- **GABA**: Magnesium from kale

5. Salmon & Almond Bowl

Ingredients:

- 1 salmon fillet
- 1/4 cup almonds
- 1 tablespoon olive oil

Instructions:

1. Cook the salmon fillet until crispy.
2. Toss almonds with olive oil and lightly roast them.
3. Serve the salmon and almonds together.

Why it's good for you: Salmon is packed with omega-3 fatty acids, which support dopamine and serotonin. Almonds provide protein and magnesium, promoting neurotransmitter balance.

Key Nutrients:

- **Dopamine**: Omega-3s from salmon
- **Serotonin**: Protein from salmon
- **GABA**: Magnesium from almonds

6. Cottage Cheese & Chia Seed Mix

Ingredients:

- 1 cup cottage cheese

- 1 tablespoon chia seeds

- 1 tablespoon honey

Instructions:

1. Mix the cottage cheese with chia seeds and drizzle honey on top.

2. Enjoy a protein-packed snack!

Why it's good for you: Cottage cheese is high in casein protein, which provides a slow-release amino acid supply for neurotransmitter production. Chia seeds add omega-3s, supporting brain function.

Key Nutrients:

- **Dopamine**: Tyrosine from cottage cheese

- **Serotonin**: Tryptophan from cottage cheese

- **GABA**: Magnesium from chia seeds

7. Turkey Lettuce Wraps

Ingredients:

- 4 ounces lean turkey breast

- 2 large lettuce leaves

- 1 tablespoon avocado (optional)

Instructions:

1. Slice the turkey breast into strips.

2. Place the turkey inside lettuce leaves and top with avocado for extra healthy fats.

3. Roll up and enjoy!

Why it's good for you: Turkey is a fantastic source of tryptophan, helping produce serotonin. Avocados provide the fats needed for optimal brain health and neurotransmitter balance.

Key Nutrients:

- **Serotonin**: Tryptophan from turkey

- **Dopamine**: Healthy fats from avocado

- **GABA**: Magnesium from avocado

8. Tofu Stir-Fry with Broccoli

Ingredients:

- 1/2 block firm tofu

- 1 cup broccoli florets

- 1 tablespoon sesame oil

Instructions:

1. Cube the tofu and stir-fry it in sesame oil.

2. Add broccoli and stir-fry until tender.

3. Serve hot.

Why it's good for you: Tofu is a complete protein, providing all the amino acids needed for neurotransmitter production. Broccoli is rich in folate and other vitamins that support brain function.

Key Nutrients:

- **Dopamine**: Tyrosine from tofu

- **Serotonin**: Folate from broccoli

- **GABA**: Magnesium from tofu

9. Peanut Butter & Chia Smoothie

Ingredients:

- 1 tablespoon peanut butter
- 1 tablespoon chia seeds
- 1/2 cup almond milk
- 1 scoop protein powder (optional)

Instructions:

1. Blend all ingredients together until smooth.
2. Pour and enjoy a creamy smoothie packed with brain-boosting protein!

Why it's good for you: Peanut butter provides healthy fats for neurotransmitter synthesis, and chia seeds offer omega-3s that support GABA and serotonin production.

Key Nutrients:

- **Dopamine**: Tyrosine from peanut butter
- **Serotonin**: Tryptophan from peanut butter
- **GABA**: Magnesium from chia seeds

10. Quinoa & Black Bean Bowl

Ingredients:

- 1/2 cup cooked quinoa

- 1/4 cup black beans

- 1 tablespoon olive oil

Instructions:

1. Combine cooked quinoa and black beans in a bowl.

2. Drizzle with olive oil and mix well.

3. Serve as a high-protein, fiber-packed meal.

Why it's good for you: Quinoa is a complete protein, offering essential amino acids for neurotransmitter production. Black beans add fiber and protein, supporting mental clarity.

Key Nutrients:

- **Dopamine:** Tyrosine from quinoa

- **Serotonin:** Tryptophan from quinoa

- **GABA:** Magnesium from quinoa

YOUR BEST BRAIN SMOOTHIE RECIPES

1. Omega Boost Smoothie

Supports brain function, memory, and mood.

Ingredients:

- 1 cup spinach (rich in folate)
- 1 tablespoon chia seeds (omega-3s)
- 1/2 cup blueberries (antioxidants)
- 1 tablespoon almond butter (healthy fats)
- 1 cup unsweetened almond milk (vitamin E)

Instructions:

1. Blend all ingredients until smooth.
2. Enjoy the omega-3s, antioxidants, and healthy fats that support your brain health and mood!

2. Memory Power Smoothie

Enhances focus and memory retention.

Ingredients:

- 1/2 avocado (healthy fats for brain function)

- 1 tablespoon flaxseed (omega-3s)

- 1/2 cup strawberries (vitamin C)

- 1/2 cup Greek yogurt (protein)

- 1 cup water or coconut water (hydration)

Instructions:

1. Add all ingredients to your blender.

2. Blend until smooth and creamy. The healthy fats and antioxidants are perfect for boosting memory and cognition!

3. Green Brain Fuel Smoothie

Packed with vitamins and minerals for cognitive support.

Ingredients:

- 1 cup kale or spinach (rich in vitamin K)
- 1/2 banana (potassium for brain function)
- 1/2 cup pineapple (vitamin C)
- 1 tablespoon pumpkin seeds (magnesium)
- 1 cup coconut water (electrolytes)

Instructions:

1. Toss everything into the blender.
2. Blend until smooth and enjoy the green goodness supporting your brain health!

4. Antioxidant Boost Smoothie

Rich in antioxidants to fight brain fog and improve cognitive function.

Ingredients:

- 1/2 cup mixed berries (blueberries, raspberries, blackberries)
- 1 tablespoon acai powder (antioxidants)
- 1 tablespoon almond butter (healthy fats)
- 1/2 cup Greek yogurt (protein)
- 1 cup unsweetened almond milk

Instructions:

1. Blend all ingredients together.
2. This antioxidant-packed smoothie helps protect the brain from oxidative stress and keeps you sharp!

5. Mood-Boosting Smoothie

Supports serotonin production and promotes a positive mood.

Ingredients:

- 1/2 cup banana (rich in tryptophan for serotonin)
- 1 tablespoon cacao powder (boosts serotonin and dopamine)
- 1 tablespoon peanut butter (protein and healthy fats)
- 1/2 cup Greek yogurt (probiotics for gut-brain health)
- 1 cup unsweetened almond milk

Instructions:

1. Add everything into your blender and blend until smooth.
2. This smoothie is a great mood booster, thanks to tryptophan, healthy fats, and serotonin-enhancing cacao!

Pro Tip: You can always customize these smoothies by adding a handful of leafy greens, protein powder, or a scoop of collagen for added benefits! Each one is designed to nourish your brain, improve focus, and support overall mental clarity.

www.ingramcontent.com/pod-product-compliance
Lightning Source LLC
Chambersburg PA
CBHW061041250726
48653CB00001B/190